EXPERIMENTING

WITH

SCIENCE

PHOTOGRAPHY

EXPERIMENTING WITH SCIENCE PHOTOGRAPHY

KEVIN AND BETTY COLLINS

AN EXPERIMENTAL
SCIENCE BOOK

FRANKLIN WATTS
NEW YORK/CHICAGO/LONDON
TORONTO/SYDNEY

To Kevin and Meghan

Photographs copyright ©: George Eastman House: p. 12 (Muybridge);
Photo Researchers, Inc.: pp. 14 (NASA/Science Source), 16 (D. W. Faw-
cett); NASA/Jet Propulsion Lab: p. 15; Henry Rasof: pp. 18, 44, 47, 50, 51,
54, 55; all other photographs copyright © Kevin and Betty Collins.

Library of Congress Cataloging-in-Publication Data

Collins, Kevin.
    Experimenting with science photography / Kevin and Betty Collins.
        p.   cm.—(Experimental science series)
    Includes bibliographical references and index.
    ISBN 0-531-11166-0
    1. Photography—Scientific applications—Juvenile literature.
I. Collins, Betty. II. Title. III. Series: Experimental science
series book.
    TR692.5.C65   1994
    778.3—dc20
                                                    93-31074 CIP AC

CONTENTS

ACKNOWLEDGMENTS

We would like to thank our children, Kevin and Meghan, for their patience in waiting for their long-promised days on warm, sandy beaches.

1

SCIENTIFIC PHOTOGRAPHY: FROM GALLOPING HORSES TO EXPLODING STARS

Scientific discoveries, technological advances, and inventions have altered human living conditions and understanding as much as any endeavor. Early discoveries in the field of electricity led eventually to the invention of radio, television, and computers. Astronomy has given us a greater understanding of the stars and galaxies. Botany, the study of plants, has shaped agriculture. Medicine, engineering, and electronics have all made our lives safer, longer, and more comfortable.

Among the great inventions have been scientific instruments, including the telescope, microscope, and artificial satellites, that have revolutionized science and expanded our knowledge of the universe. Another invention, the camera, has served the cause of both art and science, even though its initial applications were artistic.

[9]

Photography today is an integral part of modern research because of the camera's ability to document events and extend the human senses.

THE ADVENT OF PHOTOGRAPHY

The ancient Greek philosopher-scientist Aristotle (384–322 B.C.) noticed that light passing through a tiny hole in the wall of a darkened room forms an inverted image of the outside world on the wall opposite the hole. This discovery became the basis for the camera obscura, a device used by sixteenth-century artists to project landscapes onto the walls of darkened rooms. Artists could trace the projections and produce more realistic images in their sketches and paintings. When light-sensitive chemicals and special papers were developed three hundred years later, images could be captured directly on film. Photography was born.

Early cameras were crude, bulky, and cumbersome. Film, too, was hard to work with, and image quality poor. Exposure times tended to be long. In fact, the first photo, made in 1826 by Joseph Nicephore Niepce, had an exposure time of about eight hours. Nevertheless, pictures taken by some of the earliest photographers—pictures of the Civil War, for example—are as good as any taken since.

With time, the camera became a tool to accurately document the works of humankind and humankind itself. It also was used to document experimental setups and results. Since "the camera doesn't lie," scientific photographs came to have a great advantage over other kinds of scientific illustrations, which often suffered from inaccuracies.

[10]

Early scientific photography was sometimes extraordinary. For example, in 1872, before the invention of motion picture photography, an American named Eadweard Muybridge studied movement in animals. He wanted to know if the four feet of a running horse were ever off the ground at the same time. By arranging a row of still cameras to shoot in sequence as a horse ran by, he got the answer and had a photograph to prove his results. See Photo 1.

MODERN APPLICATIONS

In time, photographic chemistry and hardware were refined but the basic principles remained pretty much the same. The image of a real object can be made to form on film kept in a dark box. This principle works for mundane photography like taking pictures for passports and for highly sophisticated photography like taking pictures of supernovas—exploding stars.

While most photography done today utilizes equipment available in ordinary camera shops, scientific photography utilizes "amateur" equipment, custom-built equipment, and every combination between. Some equipment is even designed for specific experiments. NASA—the National Aeronautics and Space Administration—for instance, builds special equipment for some of its space probes.

Most photography concerns itself with visible light. Some photography, however, focuses on images produced by radiation from parts of the electromagnetic spectrum to which ordinary film and cameras are not sensitive. Scientists often use photography to extend their senses, enabling them to

Photo 1. In 1872, Eadweard Muybridge
used a row of cameras to take a
sequence of photos to determine
if the four feet of a running horse
were ever off the ground at
the same time. This photo
clearly shows the answer.

penetrate into outer space or into microworlds where their unaided eyes could not take them.

For example, NASA used a camera sensitive to ultraviolet light—the component of light that gives you a sunburn—in the *Ultraviolet Explorer*, a satellite. Scientists have used infrared photography to read otherwise unreadable old manuscripts that have faded with time. Infrared light is another form of radiation invisible to the naked eye. Writing no longer visible to the naked eye can be recorded on film as clearly as the day it was written.

Ultraviolet and X-ray photography can record the presence of stars that cannot be seen through any light telescope. High-altitude research aircraft and satellites routinely take infrared photos of large portions of the earth's surface. Using the data derived from pictures such as Photo 2, scientists can reliably estimate the condition of crops in the field, assess ripeness, and predict the potential size of the harvest.

Cameras placed in spacecraft have given scientists views of the moon and planets that were once unavailable. *Voyager 2* transmitted thousands of images during its trip toward the outermost reaches of the solar system (Photo 3). Scientists will need years to thoroughly process the information contained in these photos. When completely studied, these images may yield more information about the solar system than all earthbound planetary studies to date.

Cameras attached to electron microscopes enable scientists to probe and record images of inanimate objects, living organisms (Photo 4), and the structure of matter itself. High-speed cameras allow scientists to record the flight of hummingbirds or butterflies. Scientists can then study the photo-

**Photo 2. Aerial mapping of tree groves
with infrared photography. The lighter
areas indicate trees under stress.**

graphs to understand the intricate body movements and musculature involved.

Not all advanced scientific photography involves peering into the "invisible." Cameras and special attachments can compress time and record events that take place over time. Time-lapse photography enables us to take individual photos at predetermined units of time over hours or weeks. When viewed in sequence, the photos show us the process of decay on a forest floor or unfold the growth of a seedling before our eyes.

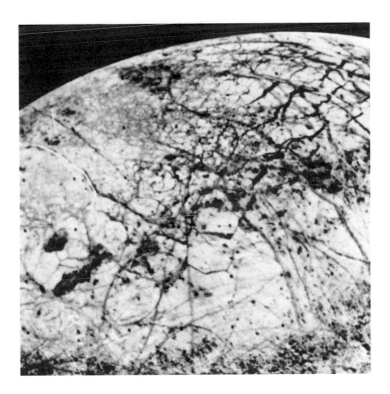

Photo 3. Close-up image of Jupiter's moon Europa taken by *Voyager* 2 from 150,000 miles (240,000 km) and transmitted back to Earth.

Interestingly, nonscientific photographers often use their cameras to reveal nature's secrets, capturing patterns in rock, birds courting, and humans expressing themselves. At the same time, scientists have taken photographs that are also artistic. One show at the IBM Museum in New York City included photographs of pollen shot at huge magnifications. These pictures were very intriguing. In a way, scientific photography had returned to its roots in the arts, while artistic

[15]

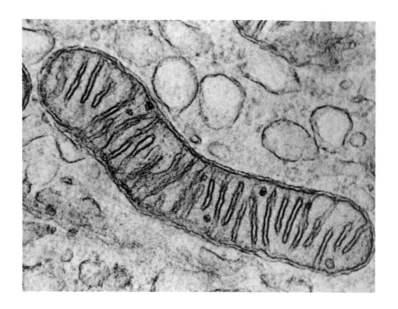

Photo 4. Photographs taken with an electron microscope make the study of intricate cell structures possible. This is a photo of a mitochondrion, the site of cellular respiration.

photography had begun to reflect the art in science!

PHOTOGRAPHY IN SCIENCE PROJECTS

With a simple camera, you can use photography as a science project or in a science project. Photography is especially useful for science fair projects, since pictures add an appealing visual component to displays and reports.

Photography can be used in all stages of a science project, from trying to decide on a topic to presenting the project at a science fair. Photography can be used in experimental procedures to record observations and document equipment set-ups, and it can be the subject of a project. It can be used in all kinds of science projects, whether experiments, surveys, displays, models, or library research. Photographs play an important role in a large percentage of science fair projects. At one science fair an observer estimated that half of all the projects on exhibit included photographs. Photos 5a and 5b show two such projects; others can be found in Chapter 3.

Chapter 2 gives more detailed applications of scientific photography.

DOING SCIENCE PROJECTS

This book contains numerous ideas for science projects along with techniques on doing scientific photography. Some of these projects are suitable for classroom or science fair projects; others are not. While some projects are described in great detail, most are not. You and your science adviser will need to decide how to best set up the project and made sure it fits your requirements.

If you need additional help, turn first to your science teacher or another knowledgeable adult and next to some of the books listed in the bibliography ("For Further Reading"). You should then be better able to choose the right project for your interests and abilities.

HOW TO BE A GOOD SCIENTIFIC PHOTOGRAPHER

As a science student, you can use photography in your projects and experiments in much the same

way as a research scientist. Depending on the equipment you have available and the time you are willing to spend, your results can be every bit as professional as those achieved by an expert. In fact, you will be an expert!

As your work through this book, keep a notebook. List the projects you have tried. Keep track of such things as the equipment and camera settings. After you have processed your film, don't forget to carefully label the photos and take notes on their quality. If you are methodical and organized, you will begin to consistently achieve good results. If your first efforts don't quite meet your expectations, do not feel bad and give up. Look over your notes, seek ways to improve your technique, and try again. Your work will improve, and you will be well on your way to developing a useful skill and satisfying hobby.

INNOVATION, A HALLMARK OF SCIENCE

Innovative thinking is one of the hallmarks of science. In fact, by its nature, science is at the frontiers of what we know and can do. This means you may have to develop new techniques to achieve

Photo 5. Photos can be used to enhance science fair displays, like these ones at a science fair in Boulder, Colorado. A good layout of photos sparks interest in the project and draws visitors in for further study.

your aims. Traditionally in science, first comes the idea, then the modification of existing equipment or the design and manufacture of new equipment to explore the idea's potential. Do not be afraid to modify or improve any technique discussed, but be sure to consult a knowledgeable adult first, to make sure what you are doing won't threaten your safety, hurt any living organisms, or ruin the equipment.

One of the earliest great innovators was Robert Hooke, the seventeenth-century English scientists who wrote the first book on using a microscope. As curator of experiments for the Royal Society, Hooke was charged with providing members with one experiment a week. To organize these experiments, he had to construct apparatus to demonstrate the phenomenon being studied. Among his accomplishments, Hooke designed or modified an air pump, a balance, watch springs, and universal joints. Robert Hooke is remembered today as much for his inventive ability as for his contributions to scientific knowledge.

The tradition of adaptability and the spirit of inventiveness continue in science today. Look at the equipment used in the explorations of the sunken ocean liner *Titanic*. Two miles (3 km) below the surface of the ocean a modified remote-control camera working on a tether allowed the exploration of the great ship's interior.

In your own work, you will probably find yourself improvising to make things work—setting up strange contraptions to get the right lighting, combining filters in a new way, experimenting with different films to get the right effect, and so on. As the old saying goes, "Necessity is the mother of invention."

SAFETY

Regardless of the type of project you do, always make safety your first priority. No photograph, however good, is worth an injury. Here are some important safety rules to remember:

- *Always work under the supervision of a science teacher or other knowledgeable adult.*
- Wear approved safety goggles in the lab and know how to use safety equipment and follow safety procedures.
- Never view a bright light—especially the sun—through your viewfinder. The lens concentrates light to a focal point, and the concentrated rays can cause permanent eye damage. If you want to photograph the sun or another bright object, build a setup so that you can photograph the reflected light.
- Keep all your equipment together so you or other people do not trip over it.
- Since a telephoto lens distorts your depth perception, never walk around while looking through such a lens. Objects close to you (such as chairs, rocks, and the edges of cliffs) will not be in proper perspective, and you may be putting yourself in great danger.
- If you photograph chemical reactions or choose to develop your own film, treat all chemicals with respect. Fumes can be toxic, and chemical burns are painful.

By following these simple procedures, you will find scientific photography an enjoyable and enriching experience.

2
PHOTOGRAPHY
BASICS

Mastering photography takes a long time, but with today's equipment, most everyone can quickly become reasonably proficient. Scientific photography ranges from easy to difficult. Some pictures are similar to those you might take for fun—for example, of a landscape, of flowers, or of people's faces; others are more complicated, for example, those of microscopic organisms.

Regardless of your level of experience, it will be worthwhile to review the material in this chapter. If you are a total novice, also look at some books on beginning photography, talk to experienced shutterbugs, read photography magazines, and, if you have the time, take a course either at your school or in a youth or adult education program.

HOW PHOTOGRAPHY WORKS

The principle of photography is fairly simple and hasn't changed much since its invention. Light strikes the film and interacts with chemicals on its surface. When the film is developed, or processed, an image appears on the film. The film is now called a negative (or a positive in the case of slide film). When the negative is printed, a positive image of the subject is formed. You now have a picture, or a print.

The *amount* of light that strikes the film is regulated by two things:

1. The size of the opening, or aperture, through which light passes from outside the camera to inside, where the film is. The aperture size is measured in f-stops.

2. The amount of time the film is exposed to the light entering the camera, known as the shutter speed.

THE BASIC EQUIPMENT

Quality photos can be taken with a minimum amount of equipment. A good beginning setup includes a 35-millimeter single-lens reflex (SLR) camera, a tripod, a small flash unit, and a flash extension cord approximately 1 meter long. The lens that comes with most cameras is adequate for most needs. Such a lens has a focal length of 50 or 55 millimeters. The focal length of a lens is determined by measuring from the film plane of the camera to the center of the lens. (Don't confuse the focal length with the earlier value of 35 millimeters, which refers to the size of the film.)

SLR cameras are either manual or fully or partially automatic. A manual camera allows you to hand-set both the aperture and the shutter speed. An automatic camera will automatically set either the aperture of the shutter speed for you. An automatic camera without a manual override may make it difficult for you to fine-tune in complex situations.

An SLR camera allows you to view your subject directly through the lens. The image is then transferred to the film as the picture is taken. A 50- or 55mm lens is most commonly used because the view seen through it approximates the view seen through the human eye. Lenses such as zoom telephoto lenses and wide-angle lenses will become useful later on, as your skills grow. Telephoto lenses have larger focal lengths (70mm+); wide-angle lenses have smaller ones (for example, 28mm).

Zoom telephotos are actually several lenses in one housing and allow the photographer to use any focal length within the lenses' range. Common ones available include 70mm–210mm and 100mm—300mm. Zoom telephotos are obviously very flexible and enable you to take good photos of distant wildlife, rock formations, and people when getting close is impractical.

Wide-angle lenses are useful in areas where space is limited or where broad panoramas are needed. If you need to photograph an electron microscope in a small office or the entire length of a cliff face where you collected fossils, a wide-angle lens in the range of a 35mm or 28mm is a good choice.

Smaller 35mm cameras, designed to point and shoot, are less versatile since you cannot control exposure times or adjust the focus. Polaroid cam-

[24]

eras also fit into this category, but you have the advantage of being able to see your photo within seconds of taking it.

Whatever camera you choose, you will get the most from it if you:

1. Know it intimately.

2. Use it regularly.

3. Make sure you understand terms such as *ISO* (which will be defined later in this chapter), *f-stop,* and *shutter speed.*

RESOURCES

Many excellent how-to books are available, including Albert Moldvay's *The National Geographic Photographer's Field Guide* and John Hedgecoe's *The Book of Photography.* These and some other how-to books are listed in the "For Further Reading" section. Kodak publishes free or inexpensive booklets on all aspects of photography. A quick visit to your local library or camera store can provide you with all the information necessary to meet your photographic needs. Talk to other photographers about equipment and techniques.

FILM

Photographs can be taken without a commercial camera but not without film. (Chapter 7 shows you how to take pictures both with a homemade pinhole camera, and without a camera at all—using film only). The type of film used affects the final image.

A quick glance at the film rack in any camera

store clearly shows that many types and brands of film are available. Each has its pros and cons: One is cheap; another expensive. One is good outdoors; another indoors. One emphasizes greens; another reds. And so on. In recent years, Kodak has introduced a number of new films, further expanding the available choices.

One strategy is to choose a film that will meet the conditions you most often expect to encounter. Use this film exclusively until you become accustomed to its characteristics and capabilities. You will then be able to use it to its best advantage. When you feel comfortable with that and ready to forge ahead, you can try some other films.

BLACK-AND-WHITE OR COLOR FILM?
Should you shoot in black and white or in color? Black and white is good in certain situations—for example, in photographing the moon. Color may be nice if the moon looks orange, but if it's a white sliver in a black sky, do you really need color? If you have access to a darkroom and know how to do your own developing and printing, you may find black and white practical, convenient, and more economical. For example, you can cheaply make large black-and-white prints where the same-size color prints would be very expensive. With black and white, you can also compensate for improper exposures, save otherwise marginal photos, and create special effects. There are several good black-and-white films, some that work well in low light and others in bright light.

Plus-X (ISO 125) is a fine-grained, medium-speed film that produces good enlargements. Tri-X (ISO 400) has been the standard film for action photography for many years. It is fast enough for action photography and when developed does not get overly grainy.

In spite of these advantages, color film is best for most needs. It captures changes in color, which are important in many projects, and—unless your black-and-white photography is stunning—has more visual appeal.

COLOR SLIDES OR PRINTS?

If after comparing black-and-white and color film you decide to work in black and white, you may want to skip to the next section.

When using color film, you will need to decide between slide film and print film. Slide films usually can be identified by the term *chrome* in their name—Ektachrome, Kodachrome, Fujichrome, etc. Print films use the word *color* in their name—Kodacolor, Fujicolor, etc.

Color print film has a good exposure latitude. That is, if by accident you adjust your camera to let in too little or too much light (one or two f-stops), the resulting photographs will not be underexposed or overexposed. Underexposed pictures are overly dark, while overexposed ones are overly light.

Slide film has a more narrow exposure latitude than print film, however. You must measure the light—using your camera's light meter or a hand-held one—fairly accurately to produce a quality image.

On the other hand, slide film can be more versatile than print film. Large numbers of slides can easily be stored and kept readily accessible. If a display is needed, quality prints can be made from slides. Slides also can be projected to form a dynamic presentation of your work for a group presentation. Slide films using E-6 processing can be developed at home cheaply and with minimal equipment.

All in all, slide film can be more economical and versatile than print film. But again, you need to experiment on your own to see which you prefer.

SLOW FILM OR FAST?

You now need to consider film speed. The speed you need depends on the amount of light you expect to have, whether the subject will be motionless or moving (and if it is moving, how fast), and the desired quality of the photographic image.

Film is given a numerical ISO (International Standards Organization) rating that is a comparative measure of the film's sensitivity to light. For example, ISO 25 film needs about twice the light of ISO 64 film to take an equivalent picture. The smaller the ISO, the more light is needed. Conversely, the larger the ISO, the less light needed. Films commonly available range from ISO 25 to ISO 1000. The higher the number, the faster the film is, and the less time it needs to capture a given amount of light.

If you are working with a subject that moves quickly (a hummingbird, for example), a fast film—ISO 200 and up—will let you use a fast enough shutter speed to stop rapid movements (such as those of the bird's wings). If you are taking pictures of a motionless or very slow-moving object in good natural light or controlled artificial light, slow film (ISO 100 or less) is fine. Rock formations, equipment setups, and close-ups of a fungus attached to a tree would all be suitable subjects for slower film speeds.

Another point to consider when choosing a film speed is the level of graininess you are willing to accept in your final photo. Grain in a photo refers to the particle size of the light-sensitive chemicals in a film.

Slow film (ISO 25 or 64, for example) contains very fine-grained substances, so the images on them are very crisp. Enlargements from these films also are clear and will make crisp photographic displays for your project. As the film speed increases, the grain size gets bigger, resulting in slides or photographs with a fine pebblelike texture, especially when enlarged.

Recent improvements have produced fine-grained fast films such as Kodacolor VR-G 200. If pollination is the focus of your study and you are trying to capture the feeding activities of insects on flowers, such a film makes it possible to freeze the insects' motion and still maintain image quality under most light conditions.

Slower films also yield photographs with more color "saturation." The light strikes the film for a longer time, allowing the chemicals in the film to develop their colors better than those in faster films.

Use the slowest film you can, given the conditions, to obtain the best-quality picture. Experimentation, again, is the only way to find out if the film you have is right for the conditions you are working in.

INDOOR OR OUTDOOR FILM?
The dyes in most films are balanced for daylight. If you are working indoors photographing equipment setups or animals in a terrarium with artificial lighting, for example, the color on your photos

will have a green or reddish cast unless you use filters on film such as Kodak Ektachrome (tungsten) that is color balanced for artificial light.

LIGHTING

There can be no photography without light. It goes without saying, therefore, that the type and direction of the light used to illuminate a subject are of great importance.

The spatial relationship between the subject and the light source has a tremendous impact on photographs. Subjects can be illuminated from the front, side(s), or back. Each has advantages and disadvantages.

Frontlighting is lighting the subject from the front. Such lighting can cast a shadow behind the subject that often gives the photograph a flat texture. When using frontlighting, you need to be especially careful not to cast your shadow on the subject.

Sidelighting is lighting the subject from the side. This type of lighting brings out the texture of a subject. Intimate details on the surface of your subject will be clearly portrayed because each little raised area casts its own shadow. Scientists studying images sent to earth by the Viking landers utilized sidelighting to get a clearer perception of the Martian surface.

Sidelighting can enhance worn or time-altered surfaces. Ancient rock carvings, called petroglyphs, are often not distinctly recorded when using frontlighting, as shown in Photo 6, which was taken in the morning. When strong sidelight is used, the shadows formed improve the image and make the details stand out, as shown in an afternoon photo, Photo 7.

Backlighting is lighting the subject from behind. Such lighting is especially useful if your subject is transparent or translucent—for example, leaves and floral parts. For best results, the light source should be diffused and not bright. A bright light can cause lens flare, which is that bright star-shaped spot of light occasionally seen in photographs. Lens flare is caused by light entering the lens at different angles and being reflected off the diaphragm of the lens.

THE GOLDEN HOURS

The most readily available light source for photography is the sun. However, problems and limitations do exist when using sunlight. Bright and direct sunlight can cause harsh shadows. Overcast days provide even lighting that is free of shadows and reproduces color well.

The best times to take pictures using natural lighting are in the morning or late afternoon. At these times, which photographers call the "golden hours," sunlight tends to have less contrast and a more complimentary tone, which gives pleasing results.

FLASH

When adequate natural lighting is unavailable, a flash unit can be used as a light source. An electronic flash unit, either built into the camera or attached to the hotshoe, or flash mount, on the camera body, produces an intense flash of light that duplicates daylight and will produce good results. If you would like additional information on

Photo 6. The frontlighting on this petroglyph, a stone carving left by ancient peoples, hides details and appears to be flat.

the use of a flash unit in close-up photography, it can be found in Chapter 4.

CONTROLLING PICTURE QUALITY

Two key factors control picture quality: exposure time and depth of field. If you have a manual cam-

Photo 7. Sidelighting on this photo, taken
later in the afternoon, gives more depth to the
picture and makes details stand out more clearly.

era, you will control these factors manually. If you have an automatic camera with a manual override, you may be able to control both of these factors yourself or sometimes just one. With some automatic cameras, both factors are controlled automatically, so you have no choice in the matter.

EXPOSURE TIME

Exposure time is the actual time the camera's shutter is open to expose the film to light. Cameras that give you at least some control have a control knob that expresses shutter speed as a number: 1,000, 500, 250 . . . 4, 2, 1, B. Each number is actually a fraction: $\frac{1}{1,000}$ $\frac{1}{500}$, $\frac{1}{250}$ . . . $\frac{1}{4}$, $\frac{1}{2}$, and 1. These numbers represent the fraction of a second the shutter is open. A shutter speed of 1,000 means the shutter is open only $\frac{1}{1,000}$ second. An exposure of 2 means the shutter is open $\frac{1}{2}$ second. The "B" setting, when used with a cable release, allows you to hold open the shutter for longer exposures.

Obviously a shutter speed of 1,000 is useful outdoors for nature photography to stop action. A shutter speed of 2 ($\frac{1}{2}$ second) is used under conditions of low light, for example, when shooting a fungus growing on the ground in a dense forest.

A shutter speed should be fast enough to eliminate any movement present as you take the picture. Shutter speeds of $\frac{1}{60}$ to $\frac{1}{1,000}$ of a second generally give the best results. For special projects, such as recording falling objects or moving parts on equipment, faster shutter speeds, such as $\frac{1}{500}$ of $\frac{1}{1,000}$ of a second, are necessary to stop any motion in your subject.

If the light meter determines that the shutter speed is $\frac{1}{30}$ of a second or longer, you will need to steady your camera to get a sharp image. This will

[34]

be necessary in low light conditions, as in night photography for astronomy projects. Tripods are outstanding for this purpose, but in a pinch leaning your camera against a steady object like a doorjamb, a fence post, or even a large rock will do quite nicely. During a long exposure any movement by either the camera or the subject will blur the image.

DEPTH OF FIELD

Depth of field is the area in front of and behind your subject that is in crisp focus at given f-stop. Depth of field is controlled by the f-stop—the size of the aperture (the opening through which light can pass)—and the distance from the camera to the subject. The smaller the aperture—that is, the bigger the f-number (for example, f-16 or f-22)—the greater the depth of field. The opposite is also true. The larger the diaphragm opening—that is, the smaller the f-number (for example f-2.5 or f-1.8)—the narrower the depth of field your photo will have. Also, the closer you are to your subject, the shallower the depth of field.

The f-stop works in conjunction with the shutter speed. When you have a fast film or a lot of light or both, you can set your camera for a fast shutter speed and a smaller aperture, giving you *maximum* depth of field. When the film is slow or the light low, you need to open the aperture to let in more light. The result is *less* depth of field.

Understanding these principles becomes important once you get to work. If you want to keep a small object in focus along with its surroundings, you will want a wide depth of field, which means a small lens opening, usually f-8 or smaller. See Photo 8 for example. On the other hand, if

your subject is surrounded by a lot of nonessential background that clutters your image, you will want a small depth of field so that you can focus on just the subject. You then will need a fairly wide lens opening, for example, f-1.8 or f-2.5. Photo 9 shows how a narrow depth of field will blur background objects and draw attention to the subject.

BRACKETING EXPOSURES

While working on your project, you may find yourself in a variety of lighting situations. For example, if your project is on the history of optics, you might want to photograph museum specimens of early optical instruments. More than likely, the instruments will be displayed in glass cabinets having internal lighting. The combination of normal room lighting, display lighting, and the reflective sur-

Facing page, top: **Photo 8. A small lens opening (f11 or f16) was used to produce this image of a scale. Notice how much of the scale is in focus.**

Facing page, left: **Photo 9. A large lens opening (f1.8 or f2.5) was used for this photo of the same scale shown in Photo 8. Notice how your eye is drawn to the portion of the picture in focus. Distracting "extra" information can be lost in the area that is out of focus.**

[37]

faces of the glass cabinets will make determining the correct exposure difficult. Light levels might be varied between bright spots and shadow areas, making your camera's light meter difficult to read.

You can use a technique called *bracketing* to help ensure success in such conditions. You use the light meter to determine which exposure is most likely to give you the desired result. You take the picture at that setting, then bracket that exposure by taking additional photographs at increments of one f-stop on either side of the main exposure.

If depth of field is critical, you also could bracket the exposure by changing the shutter speed. First, you would select an appropriate f-stop to give the required depth of field. Then you would use the light meter to adjust the shutter speed for the correct exposure. You would bracket the photo by altering the shutter speed one stop on either side of the main exposure. When the film is processed, you will have a choice of three exposures of the subject. In the case of a really important photo, you might need to bracket two stops (or shutter speeds).

SAVING MONEY ON FILM AND PROCESSING

Even if you are careful with film, the cost mounts up, especially if you are trying a new technique.

BULK FILM
A good way to begin controlling expenses is to purchase large rolls of film, known as bulk film, which is sold in 50- and 100-foot (15- and 30-m) lengths. When you buy bulk film, you prepare your

own film cassettes. The savings are considerable once you have the simple basic equipment.

A 100-foot roll of bulk film, when rolled onto film cassettes, yields about eighteen rolls of thirty-six-exposure film. The only equipment you need is a bulk loader, a supply of film cassettes, and a roll of masking tape. When loaded, cassettes should be sealed in plastic film cans and stored in a refrigerator or freezer. Film has an indefinite shelf life when stored at low temperatures. Cold film takes several hours to warm up to a usable state, so be sure to plan accordingly.

CHOOSING A LAB
According to *Consumer Reports* magazine, which rates products and services, neighborhood instant-film-processing services are the most expensive ways to process film and sometimes leave something to be desired in the quality of the finished product. Mail-order companies can be less expensive and can produce better quality.

With these types of processors, however, custom or black-and-white work may be impossible to get, so you may need to turn to a good camera shop or a professional photo lab. Although the latter can be expensive, they can also be competitive or even cheaper than other places, plus they will be able to handle special requests. A bonus is that people at these labs may take a special interest in you and your work and offer tips or go out of their way to help you get what you want. For instance, sometimes they will give you several prints for the price of one, each slightly different in color or contrast. Therefore, shop around until you find the best price and quality.

DO-IT-YOURSELF PROCESSING
You can process one type of slide film—E-6—at home. Processing E-6 slide film is fairly simple as long as you follow the directions. You will need a film reel and drum, bottles in which to store mixed chemicals, a thermometer, slide mounts, and a darkroom. Special jars or even brown juice bottles can be used. You might want to use a portable tape recorder to record the times and instructions for developing.

Processing your own slides is economical, about half the cost of commercial processing. And it is quick, allowing you to see your results in about half an hour.

MAIL-ORDER COMPANIES

During the course of your project, you may find that you need an item—a specimen or piece of equipment, for example—that is unavailable where you live. Appendix B contains a list of scientific and photographic supply companies that may have what you need. Your science or photography teacher may have catalogs from these or similar companies.

Consistently good science photography is not an accident. It is the result of a clear understanding of how a camera works and applying this knowledge to capture the desired image on film. By taking the time to master the material just covered, you will take a giant step toward becoming a proficient scientific photographer. Over time you will collect a wealth of information that will enable you to improve the quality of your photographs.

PROJECTS

1. Try films with various ISO ratings. Photograph the same image under similar lighting conditions. Compare the prints. What do you notice about grain size and color quality? How can this help you to decide on your main film?

2. Tape a poster with a print on it to a wall. Step back several paces. Start at a normal exposure, approximately $\frac{1}{250}$, and continue increasing the exposure time until you are at about $\frac{1}{2}$ second. Process the film. Lay the photos out in order. Determine what your limit of steadiness is by the clarity of the pictures.

3. Choose an inanimate subject with some depth to it. A microscope or lab balance should be fine. Explore the effect of different f-stops on depth of field.

4. Does background affect a picture? Photograph the same object using backgrounds of different colors and patterns. Does the background enhance or detract from the subject?

3
APPLICATIONS OF
SCIENTIFIC PHOTOGRAPHY

Photography can be either the center of your project or the icing on the cake. Your project might focus on your never-before-seen photographs of the life cycle of a rare insect or of the strange rock formations near your house. It might simply include decorative photographs of the plants you worked with. Or it might use photographs to document the steps of your experiment with computer chips.

USING A CAMERA TO EXTEND YOUR SENSES

One thing that all users of the camera share is that it extends the user's senses. The camera becomes an extension of your eyes and brain. Thanks to special attachments, the camera can extend one's senses to detect objects too small or faint to see with the naked eye—even objects that are invisible.

What if you wanted to photograph the tiny organisms swimming in a bottle of pond water? Or study the dividing cells in a growing plant? Perhaps you would like to record stars barely visible to the naked eye, or the tiny structures of a salt crystal.

You could do all these things with a camera and special attachments or special film. Later chapters explain how to do these things.

USING A CAMERA TO CAPTURE A SEQUENCE OF ACTIONS

Photographs are often referred to as stills, as opposed to motion pictures. The former capture motionless subjects or stop the motion of moving subjects, while the latter capture movement. However, a camera can be used effectively to record changes over time, either with or without special attachments. Photo 10 shows a science fair project that uses photographs to record the results of an experiment designed to demonstrate whether plants have feelings.

In many of your applications of scientific photography, you will be putting your camera to very good use indeed if you take a *sequence* of photographs. Here are two more examples.

You could take a sequence of photographs every hour to document any changes in the size of a bean plant. Over twenty-four hours you would probably have a series of shots that clearly show changes in height. You could plot a graph of height versus time and use the photographs to lend an exciting visual component to the statistical results.

When studying the movement of fluids within

[43]

On the display board:

IS YOUR WATER FIT TO DRINK

PURPOSE

EXPERIMENT

HYPOTHESIS

RESEARCH

DO PLANTS HAVE FEELINGS ?

RESULTS

CONCLUSION

BIBLIOGRAPHY

BVPS District Science Fair Entry Award

**Photo 10. Do plants have feelings?
The student who did this science
fair project used a camera to aid
in the investigation.**

a vascular plant, dyes are often used. The progress
of the dye within the plant can be captured on film
at regular intervals for more thorough study. This
same idea can be applied to chemical reactions.
Record the various stages of the reaction for more
complete study later. Crystal growth can be docu-
mented easily using a camera. Photographs can
be used to demonstrate the rotation of the earth
and trace the movement of the moon through the
night sky.

USING A CAMERA TO STOP MOTION

Cameras can also be used to do very unusual things—such as stopping motion. Your eye can capture a movement no faster than about $\frac{1}{30}$ of a second. A movement that is faster, for example, a hummingbird's wings in motion, will be seen as a blur. A movement that is or appears noticeably slower will appear not to be a movement at all. For instance, the moon moves so slowly that unless you watch it for a long time it will seem to be standing still.

Fast-moving objects can be "frozen" by using a short shutter speed. To demonstrate this point, watch the spinning wheels of a bicycle. You know that a bicycle wheel contains many thin spokes, but you can't see the individual spokes due to the speed at which the wheels rotate. A 35mm camera using an exposure time of $\frac{1}{500}$ or $\frac{1}{1,000}$ of a second can freeze the motion of the spokes on film.

If you want to look at the moving wings of a hummingbird or insect, you can "stop" them using very fast film, a special flash attachment, or a strobe device. You can use similar techniques for studying the motion of other animals, humans, and vehicles. Falling objects, projectiles, collisions, and moving objects in sports—for example, billiard balls, tennis racquets, and baseball bats—are all suitable subjects for photographic study using fast shutter speeds or flash units.

USING YOUR CAMERA TO CHANGE THE WORLD

You also can use your camera for good causes—such as protecting the environment.

[45]

Environmental problems like air pollution, the ozone hole, acid rain, and toxic wastes seem to be part of our daily lives, yet many people want to believe these problems do not exist or want to downplay their significance. Photographs can be used to record environmental problems. They can be the impetus to convince people to bring about change within your school or community. Photo 11 shows the exhibit for a science fair project designed to look into the effects on plants of acid precipitation.

In environmental studies, photos can portray conditions and changes more vividly than a data table. If your project is concerned with water quality and how it is affected by local construction, identify a proposed site near a stream. Photograph the stream to record its initial condition. Be sure to show the clarity of the water and the plant cover along the bank of the stream. As construction progresses, retake these same photos for later comparison.

You can also photograph dumps, roadside trash, smoggy days, auto exhaust, eyesores, etc. Always work under the supervision of a knowledgeable adult and be alert for hazards.

Photo 12 is a picture of a landfill. Photos like this one can be used to draw attention to the fact that throughout the United States such landfills are rapidly reaching their capacity.

APPLYING SCIENTIFIC PHOTOGRAPHY TO DIFFERENT TYPES OF SCIENCE PROJECTS

There are different types of science projects. Some are classic controlled experiments. Others are models or displays. Still others are surveys, or

Photo 11. Does acid rain have an
impact on plants? A camera proved
helpful in the search for an answer.

Photo 12. Sanitary landfills are rapidly filling all over the United States. Photos like this one can be used to help draw attention to the problem, perhaps providing the catalyst to starting a school or community recycling program.

fieldwork. In all kinds of scientific work, photography can be of value.

A photographic record adds not only interest to your work but also validity and visual proof to support your written results. In a competitive science fair, clear, well-mounted photos add noticeably to the eye appeal of your project and give credence to your results. What could be more appealing than stunning photographs?

DOCUMENTING EQUIPMENT AND SETUPS

A major part of any science project is documentation. You need to carefully keep track of the equipment used and how it is set up. You can photograph your equipment, including special setups. For example, if your work involves photographing fish in an aquarium, you may have to improvise a way to support flash units to clearly illuminate your specimens. You might photograph the flash setup as well as the specimens. Later you might need to duplicate the lighting setup or want to demonstrate the technique you used to a friend or teacher.

Photo 13 documents the experimental setup in a science fair project aimed at investigating the effects of automobile exhaust on plants. (*Caution:* Car exhaust is dangerous and can be deadly! If you do such a project, be sure to work outdoors and under the supervision of a knowledgeable science teacher.)

EXPERIMENTAL PROJECTS

The core of an experimental project is observations and results. With a camera, you can keep track of the conditions under which you are making observations and also record the observations themselves. When working on a project, you may be looking for patterns. Often, however, you won't notice patterns until after you have made your observations or measurements. A photographic record and careful notes will make it easier for you to look for patterns. The exhibit in Photo 14 uses photographs to document the results of the project designed to seek the effects of automobile exhaust on plants. (See previous paragraph and previous caution!)

PURPOSE

TO FIND OUT IF POLLUTION EFFECTS PLANT LIFE

Above: Photo 13. Auto exhaust, pollution, and plant health—photos document the experimental setup to determine if there is a connection. (CAUTION: If this project interests you, be sure to do it only under the supervision of a qualified science teacher.)

Facing page: Photo 14. Pictures document the results of the project described in Photo 13 and in the text.

[51]

What if you wanted to test the effects of various chemicals on the ability of the flatworm genus *Planaria* to grow two heads? What better way, if you have the equipment, than to take photographs of *Planaria* through a microscope at various stages of growth as well as before and after administration of the chemicals. When trying to determine whether light of different colors affects plant growth, you may wish to photograph the setup and plant growth at various intervals of time.

OTHER KINDS OF INVESTIGATIONS

Other kinds of investigations are experimental but may be less formal than those described above. Camera work comes in handy with these investigations as well.

For example, if you are monitoring water quality above and below a sewage treatment plant's outlet pipe, "environmental" photos of the collection sites might be useful. When separating fossils from rock layers, photos of the newly found specimens and the tools you used to split the rock could later add interest and validity to your display. In charting weather patterns, photos of sky conditions under particular barometric pressures might help you develop a system to predict weather fronts as they develop.

If your project involves trying to correlate wind exposure with tree height, you might want to photograph trees as you climb a mountain trail, showing how they become increasingly shorter as you go higher. Should your project involve the study of insect-eating plants like the Venus's-flytrap, photos of the plants before and after they have captured insects, and of the insects too, could be effective.

What if you wanted to document the phases

of the moon? How might you do this? You might describe them in words, you might draw pictures, or you might record them on film. You could take photographs every night over about one month and end up with a series of photographs showing the moon beginning as a sliver, gradually growing, then reaching fullness, and finally shrinking until it is again a sliver.

SURVEYS
Photography can help you do scientific studies such as surveys. For example, if you are doing a geologic survey in your neighborhood, you might want to collect specimens, document where you found them, and record the different types of geologic formations. You will always need careful notes; sketches may come in handy, but photographs can be a tremendous asset.

DISPLAYS
Photographs can be a major part of an exhibit-type project like a nature museum. Along with the specimens you exhibit, you can provide photographs of the places you found them. Photographs also can substitute for specimens too large to bring into the museum, like trees or rock formations. Photos can even be an entire exhibit; for instance, photomicrographs of unusual specimens such as pollen, insect eyes, and grains of sand. Photography is almost an essential part of displays and exhibits for science fairs, science museums, and school displays. Photo 15 is of a science fair project built around the subject of photography itself.

MODELS
Photos also can be used to document the steps in building a scientific instrument like a wind tunnel

**Photo 15. A science project can be
built around the subject of photography.**

or various prototype models of rockets. You might
have room in your science fair exhibit for only one
small physical model and have to provide photos
of the others, along with data, methodology, etc.
Photography is handy to document procedures
and to supplement other elements of science
projects. Photo 16 shows a science fair display that
includes a real model and photographs.

PLANNING YOUR PHOTO SESSIONS

Before you actually begin taking pictures, you
would be wise to do some planning. List the equip-

Photo 16. Photographs can be used in
science projects based on models.

ment, props, materials, etc., needed. Decide what pictures you will be taking, perhaps outlining a shooting script. This will save time and effort. A script is especially useful if you will be taking pictures in a special location where your time is limited. The script can describe the photos needed and special instructions. For instance,

1. Side photo of equipment setup for laser experiment; needs tripod, indoor film, white cardboard backdrop.

2. Top photo of setup.

3. Photo of laser on; use green filter.

The script could also include times for a shooting schedule:

12 noon: shoot bean plants outside, on patio.

3 P.M.: shoot bean plants outside, on patio.

6 P.M.: shoot bean plants inside in study, at two places 3 feet (about 1 m) apart.

It also helps to anticipate the types and numbers of pictures you need. Do you want to show a sequence over time? Will you use the photos in a science fair display or in a report? Since both of these projects have size limits, format and orientation are important. Vertical photos might work better than horizontal ones because they present a stronger image.

The script can be annotated with information gathered when you actually take the pictures. Writing the initial script can be done on a computer; that way it can easily be changed and notes can be incorporated into it later on. Captions can be prepared from the script as well.

Before even touching your camera, you also will want to read up on your subject. If you plan to investigate and photograph the life history of an insect, for example, you will want to research the subject first. Then you can more meaningfully look at the insect's activity patterns, sleeping times, and eating patterns. You will know what is important to examine and also be able to spot interesting coincidences or events.

You also may want to do extra reading on any specialized photographic techniques you will be using. You also might look at professional photos of your subjects to see how other people have treated them. For instance, if you will be photographing constellations, you will want to look through issues of *Sky and Telescope*, a magazine for amateur astronomers. If you are going to be photographing wildlife, look at nature and outdoor sports magazines such as *National Wildlife*, *Sierra*, *Outdoor Life*, *Audubon*, and *National Geographic*.

Of course, if you are doing an experiment with a hypothesis and controls, your experimental procedures will determine your photographic needs. For instance, if you are testing the effects of temperature on crystal formation, you already will be clear on the experiment and will now need to decide how to photographically record the crystal growth. You might take a picture of each setup every four hours, making sure to keep carefully written notes and maintain a photo log.

Just as creativity, accuracy, and thoroughness are hallmarks of good science, so too are they the foundation of good science photography.

GENERAL PHOTOGRAPHY TIPS

Once you know exactly how you might use photography in your science project, the same basic techniques that apply in general photography pertain to science photography. If you have a manual camera or are using manual settings on your automatic camera, check the light meter. Focus carefully. Keep the camera straight; tilted horizons are distracting. Select the f-stop with care, as adequate depth of field is important for a quality image. View the subject in both a vertical and horizontal format to determine the best way to present it.

As you work, be aware of situations or events that, if recorded on film, would help an uninformed viewer to understand your work. Don't be afraid to take pictures from different viewpoints and distances. You will be editing your pictures after they are developed and organizing them into a presentation. The more photos you have to choose from, the more likely you are to put together an interesting presentation. Film is often the cheapest part of photography. This is especially true when you are missing one or two pictures that would have really added to your presentation.

A bird hatching may require a photo every half hour. To record the molting process of an insect, you may need to take pictures every few minutes. Familiarity with your subject will help determine the proper timing between photos.

If your chosen interval is long, try to arrange your schedule so that the light will be reasonably similar at both exposures. Depending on the time of year you are working on your project, a starting point for a twelve-hour interval might be a 6 A.M.

and 6 P.M. split. This takes advantage of the softer qualities of morning and evening light.

A SAMPLE SCIENCE PROJECT WITH PHOTOGRAPHS

Whatever your interests, you might want to try a sample project before beginning the "real" thing, just to warm up. A simple project would be to document the changes that take place as a rosebud develops into a bloom. See Photos 17a, 17b, and 17c. Decide what you want to show and write it down in your journal. Then do some reading on roses. You will need some specimens, perhaps ready to bloom, or with a young bud in a position suitable for you to work with over the next several days.

Decide on the time you wish to allow between each picture. Twelve hours is a good starting point for flower development. For consistency, take all photos from the same place and at the same time, so the lighting is the same. Good times are 6 A.M. and 6 P.M., when the light is soft. Use a flash if lighting is dim or you want to "fill in." Carefully mark the spot on the ground where the tripod is placed for each exposure. You are now ready to start your sequence.

To maintain consistent depth of field, use the same f-stop for the entire sequence. The one variable you can freely alter is shutter speed. Before taking each picture, set the camera to the initial settings and then activate the light meter. Adjust the shutter speed to get the correct exposure and still utilize the chosen f-stop. The adjustments in shutter speed required to maintain the desired f-stop should not noticeably affect the quality of the photograph as long as the camera is stable.

[59]

Photo 17. This sequence of a rose opening shows how photos can be used to record an event that takes place over time and allow further study.

Knowing how to use f-stops to control the final image gives you more control over your presentation.

Record all data about this exposure: f-stop, shutter speed, lens size, and distance to subject. You can read the distance from the focus ring on the lens after it is set to take the photo.

USING PHOTOGRAPHS IN DISPLAYS AND REPORTS

Regardless of the use you make of scientific photography, at some point you will need to choose which photos to use and decide how to include them in your project.

After processing the film, go through the pictures carefully. When organizing a display for a project, choose photos whose depth of field emphasizes the key part of your image. To help select the ones that may be used, ask yourself these questions about each photo:

1. Is the image clear?

2. Does the photo emphasize key points of my project?

3. Does it demonstrate problems I had to overcome to complete my work?

If the photos are clear and to the point, you may want to enlarge some for a more eye-catching display. Check size requirements for photographs in your project before having enlargements made.

You might seek advice from your school's art or photography teacher on the best way to mount your pictures. A mat that compliments the colors in your photos will increase their visual appeal.

[61]

In order to protect the unused negatives and prints for later use, store them in file folders or envelopes that are clearly labeled according to content.

PROJECTS

1. Crystals tend to form only in fairly pure substances. This level of purity is necessary in medicine production. Test the effect measured levels of impurities have on crystal formation and photograph your findings.

2. Find out whether temperature affects the crystal formation process.

3. In order to protect the crew and sensitive electronic equipment on board, spacecraft must be protected from the heating effect of prolonged exposure to sunlight. Explore the way different surfaces absorb sunlight. What colors and textures minimize increases in temperature?

4. Soil is a mixture of broken rock particles and organic material (decayed plant and animal remains). Explore how freezing temperatures might affect the rate at which a rock surface breaks down.

5. Do seasonal changes affect plant growth? To find out, record the seasonal changes that take place in a large tree near your home. What do you find?

6. Drought or times of excess moisture place stress on plants. Maintain a daily log of moisture received and take photographs to demonstrate how plants cope with one of these environmental stresses.

7. Photograph the seasonal changes in and around a pond. Document the strategies used by plants and animals living there to survive dry times.

8. Document the changes that take place in a leaf bud as it breaks dormancy. Does a later winter storm affect a bud's ability to break dormancy? Does air temperature affect the speed at which a bud will open?

9. Study the encroaching growth of mosses and other simple plants on a rock outcrop. What patterns do you notice?

10. Study the succession of plants common in an empty lot or field over several months. What patterns do you notice?

11. Topsoil is crucial for healthy plant growth, yet it forms very slowly. Poor agricultural or construction practices can contribute to the rapid erosion of valuable topsoil. Document erosion at a local site. Develop a plan to limit the negative effects of erosion at the site.

12. Large numbers of people occupying a small amount of land often have a heavy effect on the environment. Study the impact your school's student body has on the plant life of the school grounds during the first quarter of the school year. Can you learn anything from this study about the patterns of movement of students in your school?

13. The need for a school recycling program can be portrayed by your photos of discarded soda-pop cans and reams of used high-quality paper being carted off instead of being recycled. When your photos support data revealing how many pounds of paper and aluminum are discarded each

day, solid waste disposal may become a real issue to the student body of your school.

14. Most schools offer some form of hot-lunch program. The amount and type of food thrown away each day can provide several areas for exploration. A study of the dietary preferences of your student body might provide an interesting basis for comparison to the dietary needs of third world nations. Your school's contribution to the solid waste problems could provide enlightening insights into each individual's contribution to a community problem. Your camera can provide graphic meaning to tables listing weights and types of food being discarded.

15. On a larger scale, a study of the effect that your community's solid waste landfills have on surrounding bodies of water may provide interesting data. Your work could spur a community-wide response. Increasingly, scientists are stepping into the role of using science to educate people on topics of general concern. They are working to present data in a manner that is easily understood by the untrained public.

16. Does air pollution affect the amount of precipitation an area will receive? Compare the precipitation patterns of a rural area to those of an industrialized area. Use your camera to document particulate matter in the air and other aspects of your work.

17. Our world is progressively becoming filled with noise. Microwave ovens, garbage disposals, cooling fans on home computers, and tape players all add to the background clatter. Explore how different solids transmit sound. Try to find

combinations that will minimize or deaden background noise.

18. Recent research indicates that the hole in the ozone layer is not only enlarging but may actually be spreading to the more temperate regions of our planet. This development could result in an increase in the number of cases of skin cancer. In order to minimize this possibility, people will need to become more careful about unprotected exposure to sunlight. Study the effectiveness of suntan lotions of similar SPF (sun protection factor) ratings.

4

CLOSE-UP PHOTOGRAPY—
EXPLORING IN
INTIMATE DETAIL

Just as you might use a magnifying glass to make small objects appear larger, so too can you use special camera lenses and other attachments to photograph more minute subjects. These lenses or attachments magnify objects just as do magnifying lenses. Floral parts, the intricate details of a fossil embedded in a rock matrix, the all-encompassing growth of a mold digesting a pumpkin, the wiring setup in an electric circuit—all can be recorded in intimate detail, as you can see from Photo 18.

Macro-, or close-up, photography—photography of objects and subjects close up—opens whole new vistas for exploration. The photos you produce not only can record your results but also can provide a startling display of the wonders of the natural world.

**Photo 18. By carefully cutting away
the petals of a tulip, you can take a
closer look at the reproductive parts.**

Basic photographic techniques still hold for
close-up photography, and photographs taken of
very small objects and subjects can be used for any
of the applications discussed in Chapter 3.

THE USES OF CLOSE-UP PHOTOGRAPHY

Close-up photography is especially effective for
subjects or objects about the size of a dime. They
are too large to photograph using a microscope but

[67]

would occupy only a small portion of a photograph when a normal lens is used. Anytime a subject to be photographed is too distant when the lens in use is at its closest focus setting, it is time to use close-up equipment.

The "standard" lens can focus down to about 45 centimeters (about 18 inches) from an object. Any closer and the subject appears out of focus. To see fine details, however, your camera may need to be within a few centimeters of the subject. To get this close, special lenses or accessories are needed to change the focal length of the camera. For close-up photography a number of equipment options are available, including close-up lenses, extension tubes, and macro lenses. When ease of use and economy are considered together, close-up lenses or extension tubes are suitable for most science projects. See Photo 19.

CLOSE-UP LENSES

Close-up lenses are the easiest to use and least expensive of the options available. They screw onto the front of the normal lens. No special exposure adjustment is needed. Close-up lenses are made in varying strengths (called diopters) from +1 to +10 and often sold in sets of three (for example +1, +2, +4). The larger the number, the closer you can get to your subject. These lenses can be used individually or in any combination. If you combine them, place the strongest (higher-numbered) lens closest to the 50- or 55mm lens, then attach the weaker lenses to the stronger close-up lens in descending order.

An important advantage to close-up lenses is that they can be used without having to remove the normal lens from the camera body. This may

Photo 19. Close-up attachments make it possible to move in on your subject. Shown are close-up lenses, extension tubes, and macro lens.

prove useful in rainy or dusty conditions. The main disadvantage of these lenses is that the photograph will not be equally sharp from the edges through to the center unless a small f-stop is used. Another disadvantage is that they can be used only on lenses with the same-diameter filter size. For example, a standard lens with a 55mm focal length might take 49mm close-up lenses. Another lens that can be used on the same camera body may require close-up lenses that have a different diameter.

[69]

EXTENSION TUBES

Extension tubes are hollow rings or tubes inserted between the camera body and the lens. They allow you to focus more closely to your subject than normal, and the same set can be used with any lens that will attach to the camera body. Extension tubes come in varying sizes (such as 12mm, 20mm, 36mm) and are often available in sets of three. The larger the number on the extension tube, the greater the magnification.

The tubes can be used either individually or in any combination, allowing a wide range of close-up distances to be covered. There is a certain amount of light loss when using extension tubes. As long as your camera has a light meter that reads through the lens, no special exposure adjustment is needed.

An extension tube or set of tubes equal in length to the focal length of the lens will produce a photograph with an image that is approximately life-size. For instance, if your normal lens is 50mm and you use two extension tubes of 25mm each, the final image will be life-size.

Photos using extension tubes will be equally sharp from the edges through to the center no matter what f-stop is used. A set of extension tubes can be purchased for less than $100, about three to four times the cost of a set of close-up lenses. On the negative side, since you need to remove the lens to attach extension tubes, using them during inclement weather can be a problem.

MACRO LENSES

Macro lenses are specifically designed for close-up work and usually come in focal lengths of 50mm and 100mm. A macro lens is used in place of the normal 50mm lens.

Macro lenses often come with an extension tube that, when inserted between the camera body and the lens, allows photos in which the image is approximately life-size. At this level the subject— for example, the circuitry of a pocket calculator— will occupy most of the area of the photograph.

Macro lenses are easy to use and can even be substituted for a normal lens for regular photography. They produce the clearest images of the three types of close-up options discussed.

On the negative side, macro lenses are expensive and tend to have a narrower range of f-stops than a normal lens. The maximum f-stop on a 50mm macro lens is about f-2.8, considerably different from the f-1.4 or f-1.8 available on conventional 50mm lenses.

Getting adequate light can be a problem when using a macro lens because sufficient depth of field requires at least an f-8 aperture. Artificial light may be needed.

FILM

Film choices are important because of possible equipment limitations and lighting restrictions. Close-up photography of subjects such as the fruiting bodies of lichens or the leaf structure of insectivorous plants in their natural setting is often done using available light, which, if you are shooting in a thick woods, can be minimal. ISO 200 film is reasonably fast, lets you take pictures without a tripod in most light situations, and yet has a grain fine enough to make pleasing prints.

DEPTH OF FIELD AND EXPOSURE TIME

Depth of field is critical when working close to a subject. Generally, an f-stop of f-8 or smaller is needed. When light conditions are not optimum, you can achieve acceptable results by focusing on the center of interest of your subject. The rest of the image will be somewhat blurred and draw attention to the subject.

Since small lens openings mean longer exposures, camera movement becomes a serious concern with close-up photography. When working in a lab, a small tripod is useful to eliminate camera movement. When working outside, you may need to rest your elbows on the ground or lean your camera on a rock to provide the steadiness necessary for a crisp photo.

A MACROPHOTOGRAPHY PRACTICE SESSION

Whichever close-up equipment you choose, use it often to become familiar with its capabilities, since you will need considerable patience and practice to become good at macrophotography. Start with inanimate objects and nonmoving living subjects. A few possibilities are flowers, fruits, lichens, rocks, fossils, razor blade edges, and printed letters or words from newspapers. Attach the close-up equipment and start with the lowest number or magnification. Focus as close as possible to the subject, keep the camera steady (very important in this type of photography!), and take the picture.

Continue this procedure with all the lenses or tubes, including various combinations. Keep a meticulous record of the pictures taken and lenses or tubes used. Use your results as a guide for future photos.

USING A FLASH FOR CLOSE-UP PHOTOGRAPHY

Sometimes too little light will be available as a result of weather conditions, the location of the specimen, equipment limitations, or other factors. A flash unit attached to the camera by a flash cord (1 yard or meter long works nicely) can supply the required light.

Determining the correct f-stop will take some experimentation since most flash units are designed to be attached directly to the camera and used at distances from the subject significantly longer than will be encountered in close-up photography. The flash cord allows the camera to get close enough to the specimen while the flash unit is far enough away to provide the correct amount of light.

Table 1 can be useful when you use a flash unit for close-up photography. Use the table as a starting point for determining how far the flash unit will have to be from the subject. An assistant may be required to hold the flash unit while the picture is taken. Or, if you expect to be working alone, you can use commercial brackets to hold the flash unit.

CLOSING IN ON MOVING SUBJECTS

An inanimate object is a relatively easy subject to photograph, but a moving subject is a real challenge.

Cold-blooded animals like insects, reptiles, and amphibians make interesting subjects for sci-

Table 1. Exposure table for close-up photography using a flash

Close-up lens used	Lens-to-Subject Distance	Flash-to-Subject Distance
None	Focused to closest setting	49.5 inches (123 cm)
+1	10 inches (25 cm)	28 inches (70 cm)
+2	8 inches (12 cm)	28 inches (70 cm)
+4	6 inches (9 cm)	28 inches (70 cm)

Film: Ektachrome 200   Lens: 55mm
f-stop used: f-16

ence projects. Unfortunately they are also either very active or very reclusive, making photography a challenge. A useful technique for anatomical studies is to put the subject in a loosely closed glass jar, which is then placed in the refrigerator for a few hours. Once chilled, the creature will slow down and, when placed in a natural setting (like the bark of a tree or a moss-covered rock), be relatively easy to photograph. This "chilling" slows down the metabolism of the subject without hurting it. Photographic study is much easier.

Note: If you use this technique, consult first with a science teacher or naturalist so that you do not harm the creature. Never work with warm-blooded animals this way!

A similar approach is to look for specimens in the cool of the morning, before the sun warms the animals. Most cold-blooded animals (insects, amphibians, reptiles) are more lethargic at this time because of their inability to generate and maintain a constant body temperature. A patient photographer can take advantage of both the animal's lethargy and the softer light found in the morning to produce quality pictures in a natural setting.

COPY PHOTOGRAPHY

Copy photography is a method that will allow you to use supplemental information available from other sources to enhance your science project. For example, if you want to copy a chart or photograph from a textbook to help support your project, you will have to know how to use copy photography, which is a variation of close-up photography.

Copy photography is best done on a flat surface. The page to be copied must lie flat and the camera must be perpendicular to the subject. This can be done by using an assistant or a piece of glass, large enough to cover the page, to flatten the subject.

When doing copy photography, keep the camera lens parallel to the chart or photograph. This allows for uniform clarity in your picture. Most cameras take a picture that shows approximately 10 percent more of the subject than what is seen through the viewfinder. To compensate for this, you will need to move in slightly closer to the subject than visually seems necessary. With practice you will be able to judge how much closer to move in. Your photograph will also look more appealing if it has a uniform margin or no margin at all.

A steady camera is important for copy photography. If light is abundant, hand-held photographs are possible. If light is low or many photographs need to be taken, the camera may need to be supported. A tripod or copy stand will provide the necessary stability. A copy stand is a device specifically designed for copy photography. It can be purchased, or built from plans given by Thomas F. Fuller in his *Photographic* magazine "A Portable Copy Stand" (see "For Further Reading").

Adequate light can be provided by mounting two clip-type shop lights, available in many hardware stores, at 45-degree angles to the subject. Use film balanced for tungsten light or an 80A blue filter to balance the color. Occasionally, there will be some glare from the surface to be copied. Careful use of a polarizing filter will eliminate the glare.

Use close-up lenses or extension tubes to crop off those unwanted borders. As long as what you are copying is for your own use, you do not violate copyright laws. But always identify the photo source.

AQUARIUM PHOTOGRAPHY

Another interesting way to use close-up equipment is in aquarium photography. Of course, the ideal place to photograph aquatic animals is in their natural environment, but underwater photography requires an underwater camera. On the other hand, the use of small aquariums allows the photographer to study aquatic organisms and record their behavior in a fairly realistic environment. Also, by confining the aquatic organisms being photographed in a limited space, an aquarium eliminates a problem faced by underwater photographers—the greater mobility of those organisms in their natural environment.

Suitable topics for study using aquarium photography include mating behavior of guppies, egg development of frogs, feeding behavior of tadpoles, and fungal infections on fish. See Photo 20.

The aquarium size you need is determined by the size of the organism you are studying and the number of specimens. When working with organisms 3 to 5 centimeters long, for example, two tank sizes are useful. A small tank (16 cm × 16 cm × 3 cm) is effective to study individual organisms. A tank that is twice as deep (16 cm × 16 cm × 6 cm) allows photography of a number of organisms at the same time.

It is important that your aquarium be reasonably narrow. This forces your specimen to stay close to the front glass of the aquarium and helps to minimize depth-of-field problems. If you can't buy or borrow such an aquarium, you can build your own from the plans in Appendix A at the back of this book.

SETTING UP FOR PHOTOGRAPHY
Aquarium photography requires extension tubes or close-up lenses, flash unit(s), flash extension cords, a tripod, and perhaps a flash bracket to secure the flash unit(s) in the required position. Since the flash-to-subject distance is apt to be very short, you will probably need to use neutral density (ND) filters to adjust the amount of light actually striking your film. ND filters decrease the amount of light passing through them in measured amounts, usually one, two, or three stops. These filters can be mounted on the front surface of the lens or on the front of the flash unit(s).

Possibly the best solution is to place the ND filters on the flash unit(s). ND filters on a lens make focusing difficult since they do decrease the

Photo 20. Small aquaria are helpful when photographing fish and other aquatic organisms. The limited amount of space available keeps the subject close to the camera.

amount of light passing through them. If the filters are mounted on the flash unit(s), focusing is not affected. If ND filters are not available, an alternative may be to experiment using layers of a white handkerchief placed over your flash element. This will decrease the amount of light emitted and have the same effect as ND filters.

Whichever method you use, be sure to keep detailed notes on the exposures used until you develop a suitable exposure table for your equipment. Table 2 is a sample table. Since flash units are available with a variety of light outputs, you will need to experiment to develop a similar table for the equipment you are using.

Place the organism to be photographed in the aquarium. Allow time for the animal to become accustomed to its new surroundings before you get started. If you wish, you can speed up this process and avoid shock to the subject by filling the small aquarium with water from the animal's original container.

GETTING STARTED

Table 2. Exposure table for aquarium photography using two flash units

Extension tubes	ND Filter	f-stop
12 mm	8X	f-16
20 mm	8X	f-16

Film: Ektachrome 200
Flash unit guide number: 79

Position the aquarium close to the edge of a table to make focusing easier. Mount the camera on the tripod and attach the appropriate close-up equipment.

Set the camera so that you can prefocus on the point where the specimen will be when the picture is taken. The advantage of a small tank will quickly become apparent at this point because it limits the movement of the specimen.

Use a flash for a light source to freeze any movement of the specimen. In order to provide balanced light, use two flash units. Figure 1 demonstrates the placement of flash units. Place one flash unit at each end of the aquarium. Prop the flash units firmly in place. Be sure the correct ND filters are used so that the exposure is right. Attach

[79]

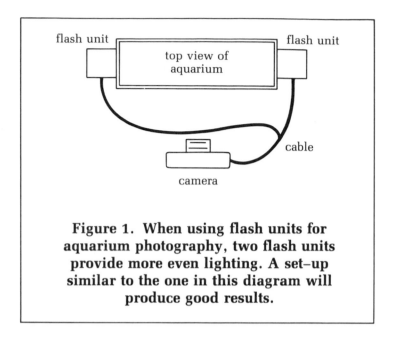

Figure 1. When using flash units for aquarium photography, two flash units provide more even lighting. A set–up similar to the one in this diagram will produce good results.

each flash unit to the camera by a flash cord so that the shutter movement is synchronized with the flash. In order to use two flash units at the same time, use a split flash cord, which allows the attachment of both units to the camera.

A potential problem with this technique is that light from a flash unit not properly aligned may cause glare across the front of the aquarium and ruin your photos. This can be corrected by cutting pieces of mat board slightly larger than the width of your aquarium. Carefully cut an internal opening in the mat board to the size of the flash lens. Attach the mat board to each end of the aquarium with cellophane tape before positioning your flash units beside the aquarium.

SPECIMEN SAFETY

Small aquariums are suitable only for photographing small organisms. Oxygen dissolved in the water can be depleted, and wastes can accumulate quickly. The specimen may become ill or even die as a result of its prolonged stay in a small aquarium. Constantly watch the subject for indications that it is in distress. If symptoms begin to appear near the end of the photo session, return the subject to its original container. If your work is not complete, use a small piece of plastic tubing to drain about half of the water out of the aquarium. Replacing this with fresh water from the original container should improve the water quality enough to allow you to finish your work without endangering the life or health of the specimen.

PROJECTS

1. Study the formation of ice crystals. What factors contribute to rapid crystal formation?

2. One step toward solving today's energy problems is to limit the waste of existing energy resources. Adequate insulation in buildings greatly reduces energy consumption. Explore the effects varying levels of insulation have on heat loss. Survey your school building for possible areas to reduce heat loss.

3. Study the shoreline of a nearby pond or lake. Do prevailing winds cause erosion?

4. Does particulate matter contained in smoke from a local industrial site impact the surrounding vegetation? If there is damage, do the prevailing

winds concentrate this impact in a particular area? Use close-up photography to document any effect these chemicals have on leaf surfaces.

5. Weather conditions can damage house paint. Does the direction a wall faces (north, south, east, or west) affect the rate of weathering? Use photography to record the evidence of weathering. Could the effect of this damage be minimized? How?

6. Investigate the role of lubrication in small-engine wear and tear. Compare poorly maintained engines with well-maintained ones.

7. Study the changes that take place in the ripening ovary of a pollinated tulip or lily. Do weather conditions affect the speed of ripening?

8. Record, on film, the methods of pollination used by local insects. Which pollinators have the greatest effect?

9. Document the life cycle of a moth or butterfly common to your area.

10. Insect infestations damage millions of dollars' worth of food crops annually. Photograph the progress of damage caused by insects on fruit trees or garden plants. Try various combinations of nonpoisonous pest controls, such as soap mixtures or solutions containing ground-up onion or garlic, to reduce insect damage.

11. Acid rain is rain contaminated by chemicals that make it acidic. When this rain falls on foliage and fills up lakes, it causes environmental damage. Compare the effects of acid rain on plants like lichens and mosses near local industrial sites and in rural areas.

12. Historically people have not been sensitive to the mutual dependence of organisms in an environment. For example, predator controls in the 1930s led to damage to the deer and moose populations they were designed to protect. Explore the biological community present in the microenvironment of a large moss-covered rock. What evidence do you find that the plants and animals living there affect each other's survival?

13. Aphids are insects that damage plants by sucking juices from their leaves. Ants are often noted to be moving among the aphids. Document the interaction of ants and aphids on local trees. How do ants and aphids affect each other?

14. Many plants drastically change their form to survive winter dormancy. Record the changes necessary to successfully cope with weather conditions.

15. Goldfish are hardy organisms that can withstand a wide range of environmental conditions. Find out if there is a connection between temperature changes and the respiratory rate of goldfish. This can be done by placing the fish in a small aquarium filled with water drawn from the same aquarium used to house them. Place the small aquarium in a larger container that has been filled with ice water. Monitor the fish's breathing rate as the temperature drops. Do not allow the temperature to drop more than 10 degrees Celsius. Document your results on film.

16. Study and photograph the various strategies used by insects in your area to winter over.

17. There are stages of development as a frog egg grows into an adult. Use aquarium photogra-

phy to record these stages while studying the feeding habits of developing frogs in a local pond.

18. Many animals are territorial. Record the effects of crowding on animals like guppies or neon tetras. Do you note a social hierarchy forming within the tank?

19. Hydra are small freshwater relatives of jellyfish. They are predators that feed on small crustaceans like daphnia and cyclops. Place hydra in a small aquarium. Study their feeding behavior, the means by which they capture prey, or their methods of movement.

20. In many states, highways are kept free of ice by spreading salt on road surfaces. Does this do anything to the chromed and painted surfaces of automobiles? Close-up photography is an ideal way to document your findings. Develop a way to minimize the damage caused by salt.

21. Landfills all over the United States are closing as they fill with refuse created by our society. Adequate ways must be found to reduce the solid waste we generate each day. Collect common containers that are not presently considered to be recyclable, such as plastics made from mixed sources or tin cans. Develop uses for these materials that will prevent their becoming part of the solid waste problem. Use photography to demonstrate the utility and effectiveness of your products.

22. Over time, rocks break down to form soil. Use close-up photography to explore the effect freezing water has on soil formation in the rocks of your area.

23. Metal fatigue has been the cause of many aircraft crashes. Explore the effect flexing has on the strength of various metals. What suggestions can you make to minimize the effects of metal fatigue?

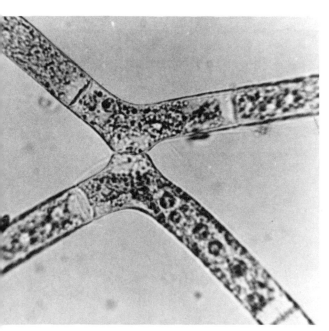

Left: Photo 22. A photo-micrograph showing the early stages of conjugation in a filamentous green alga.

Below: Photo 23. A common flea presents a whole new image when viewed through the medium-power (100x) lenses of a microscope.

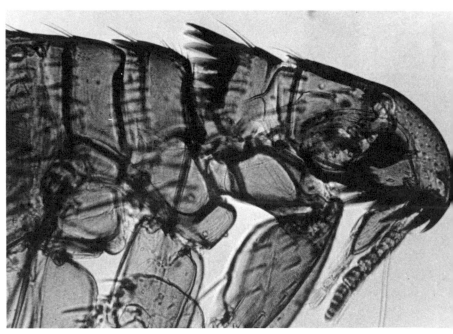

Photomicrography is more difficult with motile organisms like protozoans, since their movement tends to produce blurred images. These organisms can be photographed, but a little patience is needed.

EQUIPMENT

Photomicrography may seem complicated at first, but with a bit of effort you will soon be taking quality photos. The equipment needed is relatively simple. It includes a 35mm camera body, a microscope (preferably with an electric light source), a cable release, an adapter to join the camera body to the microscope, and a watch with a second hand.

Most microscope-camera adapters come in two parts. One joins to the camera body in place of the normal lens. The other slides over the body tube of the microscope and allows normal use of the instrument prior to taking pictures. The two parts are joined together to make the microscope and camera one unit and form a stable photographic platform.

FILM

Adequate lighting is crucial in photomicrography. Most school microscopes use a 15- to 20-watt light source, so at medium power (100x), using a slow film like ISO 25 would require an exposure time of about 10 seconds. At this speed any subject movement will produce a blurred image. If you are using a school microscope, start with ISO 200 and see how that works. Then experiment with ISO

100 and 400 until you find the speed that suits your work best.

SETTING UP THE MICROSCOPE

Remove the eyepiece from the microscope. Then slide the lower part of the adapter over the body tube and carefully replace the eyepiece.

On some microscopes, such as the Swift Model 960 or Model 3200, the body tube may be too thick for the adapter to slide over. If this is the case, you will need to contact the microscope's American distributor to find out if a tapered body tube is available. Such tubes are relatively inexpensive.

It goes without saying that if the microscope you are using belongs to your school, be sure to consult your science teacher before removing or altering any parts of the instrument.

ATTACHING THE CAMERA TO THE MICROSCOPE AND VIEWING THE SPECIMEN

Now position a slide-mounted specimen, such as a thin slice of a plant stem, on the microscope stage. Be sure to center the subject in your field of view. Remove the lens from the camera and attach the camera body to the upper part of the adapter. Join the camera to the microscope as shown in Photo 24. Look through the viewfinder of the camera to refocus on the specimen.

Most cameras have a screen that facilitates focusing in normal use. Unfortunately, this screen makes photomicrography difficult. Looking through this screen is similar to viewing a pretty scene through a screened window. The

Photo 24. Most microscope adapters have two parts. This allows the camera to be quickly attached to the microscope when a suitable subject has been found.

view is still visible, but fine details are unclear. You will need to take great care as you focus to obtain the clearest possible image.

If your camera has a split-image screen, focusing is easier. This screen appears as a circle divided in two parts in the center of the field of

[91]

view. Both halves of this circle are clear. The small amount of light available during photomicrography will often enable you to see through only one half circle at a time. If the specimen in that half is clear, the whole image will usually be in focus.

As you mount the camera and refocus, you will probably notice that the specimen appears somewhat larger when viewed through the camera than it did originally. This extra magnification is produced because the camera, when attached to the microscope, is slightly higher than your eye would be (Figure 2). To allow for the change, you will need to reposition the specimen when the camera is mounted.

The final image will actually show slightly more of the specimen than is actually seen through the viewfinder. Compose the photo carefully to make sure the final image includes no unwanted portions of the specimen.

In photomicrography, depth of field often affects image quality. On a microscope the diaphragm controls the depth of field. The smallest diaphragm setting tends to give the most detail and depth of field to the final image.

SETTING THE EXPOSURE TIME

The light source on most microscopes is below the specimen, which results in a backlighting situation. Most automatic systems are set to meter all light as though it were coming from the front of the subject. This results in an exposure error of one to two stops. With a manual camera you can adjust for the lighting but will need to make an exposure table—a guide to help you set the correct exposures.

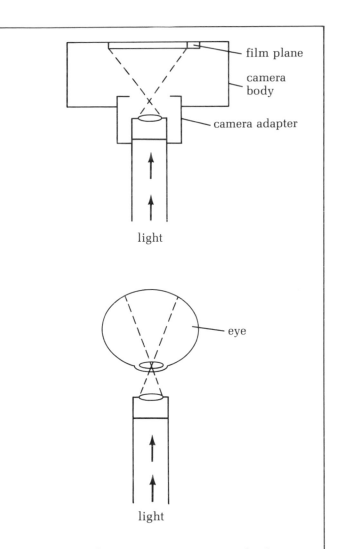

film plane

camera body

camera adapter

light

eye

light

Figure 2. When a camera is attached to a microscope, the image seen is slightly different than the view seen without a camera. After attaching the camera, the image will need to be focused again and the position of the specimen adjusted.

An exposure table is simply a set of exposures developed for each magnification present on a particular microscope using a particular speed of film. Construct this table experimentally by taking a sequence of exposures for each magnification. Then process the film to determine the best setting for each magnification.

To make an exposure table, you will essentially go through a test photomicrography session. Choose a specimen that is distinct and easy to focus on. A commercially prepared specimen of a stem cross section should work well. The cell walls are often very pronounced and facilitate producing a clear image.

Start with the medium-power lens of the microscope. Focus and position the specimen for the image you would like to record and adjust the microscope's diaphragm to a setting that gives pleasing results.

Once the specimen is ready, mount the camera, refocus, and take a sequence of exposures. Start with the exposure settings in Table 3 for the ISO used. Since the microscope and light source used may differ from the ones used to build the

Table 3. Photomicrography exposure table

Film ISO	40X	100X	400X
50	½ second	4 seconds	32 seconds
100	¼ second	2 seconds	16 seconds
200	⅛ second	1 second	8 seconds
400	¹⁄₁₅ second	½ second	4 seconds

Microscope used: Swift Model 950 with built-in illuminator
Diaphragm setting: No. 1 (smallest opening)

table, bracket all exposures. For example, if the table recommends an exposure of 1 second at medium power using ISO 200 film, take three exposures of the same subject (½, 1, and 2 seconds).

AUTOMATIC CAMERAS

With an automatic camera, you can compensate for the backlighting problem in one of two ways. If the camera has an override function to allow for backlighting, use it each time you take a photomicrograph. If not, you may need to "fool" the automatic system by resetting the ISO to allow for the necessary increased exposure. Once you have learned how to use the automatic features on your camera for photomicrography, no exposure table is necessary.

For example, if the film is ISO 200, set the camera at either ISO 100 or ISO 50. Initially, you may need to shoot pictures at all three settings to determine which gives the best results. This procedure corrects for the backlighting that exists when the light source is under the specimen. No special processing will be required when the film is developed. After the photomicrography session, return the ISO to the true setting. Otherwise, if used for conventional photography, all the photos will be overexposed.

MANUAL CAMERAS, OR AUTOMATIC
CAMERAS WITH MANUAL OVERRIDE

Manual cameras have no automatic functions, and some automatic cameras have a manual mode. As the photographer you will have to—or can—physically make all adjustments for the exposure time of each photograph. It is useful to make an expo-

[95]

sure table for photomicrography similar to the one in Table 3 as part of your initial work and then base all subsequent exposures on that table.

A PRACTICE PHOTOMICROGRAPHY SESSION

Let's run through a practice session using the wing of a fly as a specimen. Be sure the microscope adapter fits both the camera body and the microscope. Keep the cable release handy. Attach the bottom half of the adapter to the microscope and the top half to the camera body.

Mount the specimen on a microscope slide, preferably in water for a clearer image and covered with a glass cover slip so you can use the high-power lens if you choose to. Place the mounted specimen on the stage of the microscope, adjust the diaphragm to the opening which provides the best view of the subject, and examine it thoroughly. The smallest diaphragm setting gives the most depth of field and produces the most crisp photographs.

Once you have found the part of the specimen that you wish to photograph, move this part to the center of your field of view. Carefully attach the camera to the microscope. Adjust the specimen so that it looks the way you want it to and refocus to correct for that adapter. Attach the cable release to the camera.

For a manual camera you will need to develop an exposure table specific to the equipment you are using. Use the exposure times found in Table 3 as a starting point for the ISO film you are using. For your first photos be sure to bracket the exposure indicated in the table because the microscope you are using may have a light source with a different intensity. Take the photos. Record pertinent information in your notebook.

Follow this procedure for each microscope lens you wish to use. When you are done, clean up and put the microscope away. Finish the roll of film on some other aspect of your science project.

When the film is processed, go through the images and check your results. When you view the photomicrographs in the order they were taken, you will be able to determine which exposure is the best for each diaphragm setting and microscope lens combination.

In the early stages of your work, be cautious. If the specimen is difficult to obtain or crucial to your project, take several exposures and bracket the main exposure suggested by your table. While this practice may seem wasteful, imagine your frustration should the one photo that is core to your work be ruined by specimen movement or an incorrect exposure. With photomicrography, redundancy of exposure is a good rule of thumb.

FLASH PHOTOMICROGRAPHY

Plant cells and fixed specimens of microorganisms pose no problems in photomicrography. However, there will be times when you wish to study an organism that is active or whose internal parts move rapidly. You also may wish to study physical processes—for example, crystal growth or Brownian motion (the vibration of small particles due to molecular movement)—in which motion could be a problem. Normal exposure times lead to blurred images. More light is needed to enable the use of faster exposure times.

One way to increase the available light is to

use a brighter light source, such as a slide projector light. This light can be reflected into the microscope's lens using the mirror. Such light may be so intensely bright that it is difficult to work with. Sunglasses are one solution to the problem.

Alternatively, an electronic flash unit can be used with a microscope to provide quick bursts of light that stop motion. An apparatus can be constructed that allows the microscope to work under normal lighting conditions but illuminates the specimen as the photo is taken. This device is easier on the eyes and still freezes motion.

To construct a flash attachment for photomicrography, you will need an electronic flash unit, an extension cord to join the camera to the flash unit, several neutral-density (ND) filters, tape, a small piece of window glass, and a supply of lightweight cardboard. Build a rectangular cardboard box, open at both ends, with a side opening to allow placement of the electric light source. Insert the piece of window glass into the side opening at a 45-degree angle so that light is reflected to the microscope's mirror, as in Figure 3. Fit the flash unit snugly into the opening of the box farthest from the microscope. Attach the flash unit to the camera body with the extension cord.

Synchronize the exposure time with the flash unit (usually 1/60 of a second). Use a cable release to take a photo when you are ready. The obvious question is, how do you adjust the amount of light to provide the correct exposure?

Photo 25 is a flash micrograph of a group of the protozoan *Euglena*. The flash unit stopped all movement and made possible a clear photo of the organism.

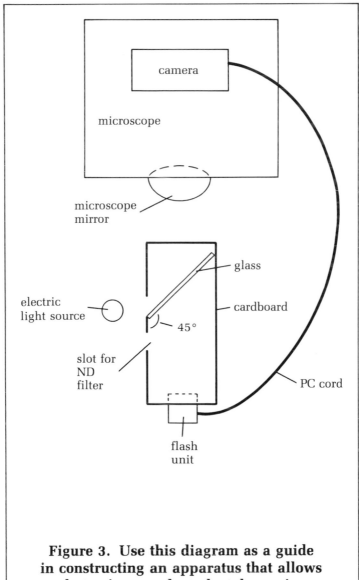

Figure 3. Use this diagram as a guide in constructing an apparatus that allows photomicrographs to be taken using a flash unit as the light source.

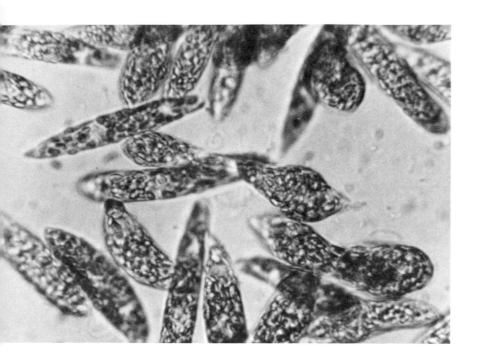

Photo 25. A flash photomicrograph of a group of the protozoan *Euglena*. The flash unit stopped all movement and made it possible to have a clear photo of the organisms.

EXPOSURE

Use ND filters and develop an exposure table. ND filters were mentioned in Chapter 4 and are used to decrease the amount of light hitting the film surface. They are available as solid squares or flexible plastic films. By cutting an opening in the cardboard flash attachment between the flash unit and the piece of glass, you can insert an ND filter or filters of the appropriate strength. If flexible ND filters are your choice, they can be attached directly to the front of your flash.

To determine the correct exposure, take a series of photos. Start with the medium-power microscope lens and set the diaphragm to the size you are most likely to use. Take the first photo without any filter; then use exposures with $2\times$, $4\times$, and $8\times$ (or 1-stop, 2-stop, 3-stop) ND filters. Process the film and determine which exposure produces the best pictures.

Table 4. Exposure data for flash photomicrography

Power	ND Filter
$100\times$	$8\times$ and $2\times$
$400\times$	$8\times$

Film: Ektachrome 200
Diaphragm setting: No. 1

You should now be able to predict which filters are necessary for the low- and high-power lenses of the microscope. On a second roll of film, test your predictions for low and high power, bracketing each exposure to make sure you get good results. When the film is processed, you will have an exposure table similar to the one in Table 4 and be ready to use flash photomicrography in your research.

PROJECTS

1. Contact the geology department of a college or university to see if you can obtain thin slices of various rock samples (granite, gneiss, etc.). Document crystalline structure in each. What does the crystalline size and structure tell you

about the geologic history of the area where the rocks were formed?

2. With the renewed interest in the construction of a space station, long-term American occupation of space may become a reality. Any living organism needed on the space station must first survive the stress of launch. Estes, a model-rocket company listed in the resources section of this book, markets rockets capable of carrying a cargo. Use one of these rockets to test the effects of rapid acceleration on small invertebrate animals, such as *Paramecium, Daphnia,* and insects. When using model rockets, be sure to follow the safety procedures provided by the manufacturer.

3. Obtain samples of sand from several locations. Examine each sample for evidence of microscopic life such as pieces of skeleton or shells from protozoans like foraminiferans. What do the items you find tell you about the biological history of the area?

4. Use photomicrography to investigate plankton, whose small size and transparent skeletons make studies in body development and embryology possible. You can maintain plankton in a small container and do your work at home.

5. Microscopic organisms form the base of the food chain in bodies of water. Often the interactions of these organisms are poorly understood. Collect a water sample from a local pond or ditch. Include either bottom mud or partially decayed plant matter. Study and document on film the succession of plant or animal life over a period of weeks.

6. Obtain a pure culture of a protozoan such as *Paramecium*. Mix dilute samples (such as 10:1 or 20:1) of common substances such as coffee, tea, and soda, respectively. Add the solution to slides with paramecia. Photograph the organism before, during, and after the process.

7. Explore the effects of variations of temperature on protozoan populations. At what temperature does the culture grow best? At what point does the culture begin to die off? How can your results be applied to the area of a river where water used to cool machinery is returned?

8. Obtain a sample of small freshwater crustaceans such as *Daphnia*. Observe the changes that take place as food passes through the digestive system of a daphnia. Does environmental temperature affect digestion?

9. Many freshwater planktonic organisms, like *Daphnia* and *Cyclops*, have never been thoroughly studied. Record the complete life cycle of such an organism on film.

10. Diffuse a dilute solution of tobacco tea made from a cigarette soaked in water across a microscope slide containing daphnia. Photograph the effects.

11. Stomata are leaf structures that control the passage of gases in and out of the leaf. Collect deciduous plants from moist and dry environments. Compare the number of stomata per unit area present on each. How do the numbers of stomata present on plants' leaves control water loss? Can your results be used to predict the kind of environment a plant of unknown origin inhabits?

12. Start seeds of easily obtained plants like beans and corn in a variety of soils (such as clay, humus, sandy soil). When the plants have grown for several weeks, study the variations in root development, including longitudinal slices of root tips. Rough longitudinal slices can be made by laying the root on a flat surface and cutting lengthwise through the root with a new single-edge razor blade. This will produce a specimen which can be mounted on a microscope slide and examined or photographed using 40x or 100x magnification. If you have access to a microtome, a device used to make thin sections for microscopic study, longitudinal sections can be more easily made. What factors contribute to the development of a healthy root system?

13. Mix saturated solutions of chemicals like sodium chloride or potassium permanganate. Photograph crystal formation and growth over time. Use these observations as the basis of a project.

14. If you have access to a university with a department of marine biology obtain marine bottom sediment samples from different depths. Document and compare the animal specimens contained within each.

15. Study digestion in organisms such as *Paramecium*. What factors control the digestion rate?

16. Peristaltic movements are the muscle contractions that move food through the digestive system. Study these movements in the digestive system of *Daphnia*. What role do muscle movements play in the breakdown of food?

17. Compare the plankton populations of a pristine pond or lake with those of a polluted pond

or lake. Note the variety and population of individual organisms in each body of water. Do pollutants affect these populations? If so, how?

18. Study the embryological development of snail eggs using egg masses found in an aquarium. What effect do dilute solutions of common wastes, such as soap and petroleum compounds, have on embryo development?

19. Use a paste of boiled cornstarch and water as a growth medium to study the germination of mold spores and formation of a mycelium. What factors control mold growth?

20. Soil fertility is often affected by microscopic animals living within it. Animals like nematodes (roundworms) and various protozoa are quite common. Obtain samples of soil from several environments, such as a garden, lawn, or a dirt parking lot. Do the numbers of animals found in each sample form a pattern that can be used as an indicator of soil quality?

6

ASTROPHOTOGRAPHY AND INFARED PHOTOGRAPHY— LOOKING INTO FARAWAY OR INVISIBLE WORLDS

A 35mm camera has unique applications in science photography. Its ability to collect light on film allows you to photograph faint stars invisible to the naked eye. Additionally, astronomers have long known that stars emit different wavelengths of light, depending on their temperature. Our eyes are not sensitive enough to notice these differences, but by using color film and a long exposure, the colors can be recorded on film. This extension of your senses will give your work added visual appeal and draw attention to your results.

ASTROPHOTOGRAPHY

Astronomy is one of the few sciences where amateurs are actively involved and working cooperatively with professionals. There are worldwide networks of volunteer organizations working jointly to monitor and explore the night sky. Astrophotography, photography of the night sky, isn't limited to observatories with large telescopes.

Several star guides are available to help you become familiar with the night sky. As your study progresses, you will develop a skill that links you with astronomers and explorers of the past. The night sky today looks much the same as it did in the time of Columbus, Galileo, and Copernicus.

For constellations and general night photography, a 35mm camera with a standard lens, a tripod, and a cable release are all the equipment you need.

Obviously, the best place to take sky pictures is away from all light. Suitable places for astrophotography include remote mountain, prairie, or beach areas, where dust and light pollution will not cause problems. One of the drawbacks of modern civilization is the large amount of light generated each night. Towns and cities are literally covered by a dome of light that can obscure all but the brightest stars. Many urban dwellers are deprived of the age-old pleasure of witnessing the stars' progress through the sky. If ideal conditions are not available, take advantage of darker areas nearby that are void of major light sources.

Astrophotography is a broad field. Anything visible in the sky at night can become a focus for study. The moon, constellations, meteor showers, satellites, star trails, aurora displays, and various other celestial phenomena are all suitable topics. However, weather conditions and their effect on the night sky make flexibility an important characteristic for an astrophotographer.

Use your notebook to keep track of your subjects, the weather conditions, and the camera settings used. This information will be helpful in evaluating your images and producing dependable results on future outings.

PHOTOGRAPHING THE CONSTELLATIONS

When working with people newly interested in the night sky, astronomers refer to the need to "know sky." The major constellations literally form a map that can be used to locate other celestial objects. Photo 26 shows the Big Dipper.

You will need a camera capable of manual settings, since too little light reaches the camera from celestial objects to have much effect on the light meter.

Black-and-white film gives acceptable results, but color film produces more interesting photos because it can record the different colors of various stars. Start with ISO 100 to ISO 400 slide film. Print films can be washed out in processing, since the processing equipment adjusts the color for a "normal" exposure—astrophotographers are not "normal." Slide film is not corrected in processing, so color and exposure are more accurate. Prints can then be made from your slides. However, if you prefer print film, request hand processing and attach a note explaining what types of photos are on the film. Special processing may or may not be available at local quick-developing services.

Once you have familiarized yourself with some of the constellations, try photographing some of your favorites. Point the tripod-mounted camera at the subject. Set the focus ring on infinity and use the widest f-stop. Set the exposure at "B."

Photo 26. The Big Dipper makes a suitable subject to start your explorations of astrophotography.

Using the cable release, hold the shutter open for 20 to 60 seconds. Then release it.

You can build an exposure table for astrophotography in much the same way you did for photomicrography. To ensure quality results and conserve film, make the exposure table before starting a serious project.

When arranging your equipment, use the minimum amount of light possible to set up. Once the equipment is ready, turn off the lights and wait several minutes to allow your eyes time to adjust to the darkness. This will make it easier to find the stars or group of stars you want to photograph. You may need to use a bright star as a kind of guide to find the dimmer ones.

STAR TRAILS—RECORDING THE EARTH'S ROTATION

The earth's rotation is hard to detect with our senses alone, but evidence of the movement can be recorded on film. This movement centers on a point in the sky called the celestial pole. By coincidence, the North Star is located approximately at this point. All stars in the Northern Hemisphere appear to move around the celestial pole. The closer a star is to the polestar, the smaller

Facing page, top: **Photo 27. By taking a 1½-hour exposure, the rotation of the earth is readily seen in this star trace. The trees in the foreground add interest to the photo and emphasize the stability of the camera.**

Facing page, bottom: **Photo 28. This star trace resembling the patterns of Morse code is both interesting to look at and clearly shows the difference in brightness of different stars present.**

the apparent motion. The farther away from the pole, the larger is the circular path a star takes, with some star paths actually dipping below the horizon.

To photograph the circular path of the stars, point the mounted camera tripod so that the North Star is near the center of your field of vision. With the exposure setting on "B" and a wide diaphragm setting (f-1.8 works well), use a cable release with a locking mechanism to hold the shutter open for 1 to 1½ hours. Photo 27 demonstrates the potential results.

Your photo will actually show the apparent path the stars traveled as the earth rotated on its axis. You will also be able to see the color and approximate brightness of stars in your field of view.

There are various ways to creatively apply this same basic idea. Open the shutter for 40 seconds, then carefully place a lens cap on the still-open lens for about 5 minutes. Remove the lens cap and repeat the sequence. You get a unique star trace reminiscent of Morse code as seen in Photo 28.

PHOTOGRAPHING AURORAS AND LIGHTNING

A similar technique can be used to record auroras and lightning. An aurora is glowing light, visible in the night sky, produced in the earth's atmosphere by impacts of charged particles from outer space. It often resembles a foglike glow and comes in many forms and colors, red and green being the most common. Sometimes auroras can be seen as vibrating or pulsating bands or arcs. Aurora displays are usually visible in the late fall or the winter because the nights are longer and the air tends to be less hazy. The aurora borealis, a particularly spectacular aurora display, can generally be seen in the northern portions of North America, Asia, and Europe.

Film and lens requirements when recording auroras and lightning are the same as when photographing the constellations. Mount the camera on a tripod and focus at infinity. The lens should be wide open (approximately f-1.8) and the exposure set to "B." Exposures from 20 to 60 seconds should yield acceptable results.

For lightning, the setup is the same as for an aurora except that the lens should be set to f-8. The shutter should be held open using a cable release for a series of lightning strikes. By pointing the camera at the part of the storm where lightning activity is evident, exciting results can be obtained, as in Photo 29.

Caution: Always work under supervision of a knowledgeable adult when photographing lightning. You can be killed by a direct lightning strike or by a falling tree or branch struck by lightning. Avoid high vantage points and tall objects like trees or power poles that can act like lightning rods. Stay away from areas where lightning strikes are very near. If your hair begins to stand on end, a strike may be imminent. Quickly get to a low place, curl up in a ball, and cover your head.

PHOTOGRAPHING THE MOON

Lunar studies present many photographic opportunities for a person interested in astronomy. The moon passes through several phases in its monthly cycle. These phases can be captured on film.

Unfortunately, you need access to a large lens

Photo 29. By pointing a camera at the center of a lightning storm and using a cable release to hold open the shutter for several bursts of lightning, exciting images can be made. Be sure to follow the safety precaution in the text before trying to photograph lightning.

to capture an impressive image of the moon. Any lens with a larger focal length than 50 to 55mm is considered a telephoto. Even with a medium-size telephoto lens (such as 100mm), the moon will appear only as a bright spot on your photo.

If you have access to a large telephoto lens, determining the correct exposure for lunar photography is a challenge, since standard light meters can be fooled. The combination of a dark night sky and the bright reflective surface of the moon causes most light meters to average the scene. This leaves the night sky muddy looking and the moon over-exposed.

Fortunately, the solution to this problem is relatively easy. The light coming from the moon originates from the sun and is reflected to the earth by the lunar surface. Essentially you are viewing a sunny surface.

You can apply what photographers call the "sunny 16" rule. On a bright, sunny day, set the lens at f-16 and your exposure time will be the setting closest to the ISO of the film you are using. For example, if you wish to shoot a picture of the full moon using ISO 400 film, set your exposure time to $\frac{1}{500}$ (the exposure time closest to 400) and use f-16. For a half-moon, the exposure needs to be longer, $\frac{1}{125}$, because light is decreased. The exposure for a crescent moon needs to be even longer: $\frac{1}{30}$ would be a good starting point. Like any rule in photography, this is an approximation. You will get more dependable results by bracketing your exposures.

AERIAL PHOTOGRAPHY WITH A ROCKET

Scientists sometimes survey populations of animals from aircraft. By taking aerial photos in a single pass over a nesting or feeding area, they record data quickly and do not greatly disturb the animals. The resulting photographs can be analyzed in the comfort of the lab, and the data they provide are available for further interpretation at a later date.

Satellites are also used to assess crop production, to inventory natural resources, and to monitor environmental degradation. Aerial photos add a perspective that lends itself nicely to many science projects. The problem for student researchers is how to economically obtain aerial photos of the area being studied and the data they can provide.

A relatively simple system exists that makes aerial photos available inexpensively while providing fun at the same time. Estes, a company that produces model rockets and components, manufactures a rocket called Astrocam 110 (Photo 30).

The nose cone of this rocket is actually a camera that uses 110-size, ISO 400 print film. The instructions provided with the kit outline times of day and light conditions necessary for proper exposures. These instructions should be followed carefully to obtain satisfactory results.

Astrocam takes one photo per flight. By using a variety of engines and launch angles, good photos can be obtained of most subjects. The camera has a simple design and is very sturdy, a point that is comforting when a hard landing occurs. The major drawback to the system is the lack of control over when a photo will actually be taken. Essentially, the shutter is released just before the parachute is deployed. The area the nose cone is pointed at during that moment will be captured on film (Photo 31). If there is a particular photo you want, be prepared to launch several times to obtain acceptable results.

If the place where you wish the rocket to land is small, the high altitude reached by a large engine may allow too much time for the rocket to drift as it floats back to earth. Do not be afraid to experiment. Try replacing the parachute with a streamer. This will let the rocket fall more quickly and minimize drift.

Right: Photo 30. An Astrocam 110 rocket on the launchpad ready for a flight. This rocket is capable of taking one aerial photo each flight.

Below: Photo 31. Photo taken using Astrocam 110. To get usable results, it is important to closely follow the manufacturers' instructions.

Since model rocket engines are made in a variety of sizes, another alternative is to utilize smaller engines. By launching Astrocam 110 at an oblique angle with a smaller engine, you may obtain a photo showing more of the ground area. The lower altitude attained by the smaller engine will give you more control over where your rocket lands and hence increase your chances of recovering the whole system.

Since whatever goes up does not always come down where you would like it to or in reusable condition, it is helpful to know that Estes will let you order spare parts to repair damage to your Astrocam 110.

Safety note. When using model rockets, always work under the supervision of a knowledgeable adult. Carefully read the guidelines provided with each kit and follow the instructions fully. Be especially alert at the time of launch to make sure that the area around your launcher is clear of people and that there are no obstructions overhead that might interfere with your rocket's flight. Do not modify the rocket unless you are following the manufacturer's directions.

High winds or rain may force the launch to be postponed. Using a model rocket will make you far more sympathetic to the delays NASA sometimes has to contend with before a mission can begin.

INFRARED PHOTOGRAPHY

As you probably know, light is a form of radiation composed of many wavelengths. The portion of this radiation that we can see is called the visible spectrum. Ordinary photography deals with light in the visible spectrum. Another type of radiation, known as infrared, exists beyond the red end of the visible spectrum. Special films sensitive to infrared enable you to explore areas and phenomena not normally available to our senses.

Conventional color film has three layers of emulsions—red, green, and blue. Infrared film also has three layers of emulsions, but they are red, green, and infrared. Using infrared films gives a "false color" image. For example, the green leaves on healthy plants appear red on an infrared photo, while the leaves of environmentally stressed plants appear yellow, green, reddish purple, or brown. In other words, signs of stress invisible to the ordinary observer are rendered visible by infrared photography. See Photos 32a and b.

Infrared photography requires the use of filters, since infrared film is also sensitive to visible light. For black-and-white infrared film, a red Kodak Wratten Filter No. 25 will decrease the amount of visible light striking the film while still allowing visual focusing. For color infrared film, a yellow Kodak Wratten Filter No. 12 has the same effect.

Infrared light has a longer wavelength than visible light, so focusing is slightly off when using infrared film. Many lenses have a mark on the focusing ring to adjust for infrared film. The photographer focuses on the subject in the normal manner and then, before making the exposure, realigns the focus setting with the infrared mark. In the event that a lens does not have this mark, the photographer can focus as usual, adjust the exposure to use a small lens aperture (f-11, f-16, or f-22), and use depth of field to compensate for the difference in focal point.

Outdoors, sunlight can be used as a light source for infrared photography. The amount of

[119]

Photo 32. Top: photo made using infrared film and a red No. 25 Wratten Filter. The portion of the leaf infected with a fungal growth gives off different light wavelengths than the healthy portions of the leaf. Bottom: photo made using standard black-and-white film. The infected areas do not show up as distinctly as they do in the infrared rendition.

infrared light available can vary greatly depending on the cloud cover or the amount of haze present. Unfortunately, light meters are not normally sensitive to infrared radiation. Use the instructions contained in the film packaging to help determine the correct exposure.

Indoors, electronic flash units will provide a suitable light source. For best results the light must be evenly spread over the subject. For small subjects this can be achieved by using two flash units equidistant from the subject and mounted at 45 degrees from each other. On larger subjects four flash units should be used.

Fluorescent lighting is not an acceptable light source since it emits no infrared radiation. Photoflood lights can be used but because of the difference in color balance of the light they emit and the daylight-balanced infrared film, results will be more acceptable with electronic flash units.

APPLICATIONS OF INFRARED PHOTOGRAPHY

Infrared photography has myriad scientific applications.

In agriculture, plants under stress give off different wavelengths of infrared light than healthy ones. When captured on infrared film, this information provides researchers with an early detection system on the health of crops in the field. When infrared aerial photos are used, scientists can assess ripeness and potential yields of crops still in the field.

In medicine, because infrared energy penetrates 2 to 3 millimeters into the skin, infrared photography makes it possible to study blood flow and surface circulatory blockages. Infrared color film is also helpful in circulatory studies because it records venous blood as a reddish brown and arterial blood as a greenish brown. Diseases like cirrhosis of the liver and breast cancer, as well as subsurface tumors, affect surface circulation. Picture sequences taken over a time span can give valuable information about the progress of those conditions.

Forensic scientists and archaeologists use infrared film on objects or documents whose inscriptions or print has faded or perhaps been altered. Writing that is not legible to the naked eye can be read when photographed by infrared film. Many ancient texts, the Dead Sea Scrolls, for example, have been read and reconstructed with the aid of infrared film. Forged documents or altered works of art can often be exposed using infrared photography.

Unfortunately for most readers of this book, the infrared studies commonly seen in science specials showing variations in heat from different portions of the human body are possible only with electronic equipment unavailable to the average amateur scientist.

The types of infrared photography already discussed do provide science with a readily accessible tool for extending our senses. Because it can be utilized with inexpensive equipment, infrared photography is also a suitable tool for the amateur scientist.

PROJECTS

ASTROPHOTOGRAPHY

1. Using Astrocam 110, observe the impact of people walking and sitting on the lawn surround-

ing your school. Study their effects on ornamental vegetation. Develop a plan to minimize any negative impact you may notice.

2. The shutter of Astrocam 110 is difficult to control. It may not always be possible to obtain a photo of a specific area. Design a means to take aerial photos using a kite or radio-control airplane as your photo platform. Will your platform allow more precise control of the image of your subject?

3. Using aerial photography, monitor patterns in stream flow in a local stream or river. How does moving water shape the surrounding land? Is erosion taking place at some sites and not others? Why? What effect does the speed and amount of water have on the vegetation of an area along the bank? Be careful to choose your launch and landing sites well. Wet film produces poor images.

4. Many comets and celestial events are actually first noticed by amateur astronomers. Contact an astronomy club in your area for information as to how you can become part of their night sky observations. Choose one particular section of the night sky and photograph it regularly over a period of time. Do you notice any unexpected changes in the area of sky you are monitoring?

5. If you have access to a larger lens, record the phases of the moon or a lunar eclipse. What effect does atmospheric haze have on the quality of your photos?

INFRARED PHOTOGRAPHY

6. Do automobile emissions have an effect on plant life growing on roadsides? Use infrared film to record the foliage of plants close to and far from

the highway. What differences in plant health do you note?

7. Infrared radiation penetrates the skin about 3 millimeters deep. This fact makes it possible to study the effect of substances such as coffee, tea, or colas on the circulation in blood vessels just below the skin surface. How much of each of these substances must be ingested before surface blood circulation is affected?

8. Compare the condition of plants growing in an industrialized area to similar plants in a more rural area. Do any differences in plant health that were not visible to the naked eye show up by using infrared photos?

9. Using infrared film, photograph an annual plant as it passes through its entire life cycle. What changes do you note in the infrared radiation reflected by the plant at various stages of the cycle?

10. Using the photo platform you developed in project 2 and infrared film, study the overall health of plant life in the area surrounding your school or home. What evidence do you find of plants under stress due to the influence of people?

11. Infrared film can be used to identify point sources of water pollution, such as a sewer outlet draining into a body of water. Use the photo platform you developed in project 2 to study the health of small bodies of water in your area.

7

SCIENTIFIC PHOTOGRAPHY WITH LIGHT-SENSITIVE PAPER AND PINHOLE CAMERAS

You can do science photography without a manufactured camera. How is this possible? By using special light-sensitive paper without a camera or by using a homemade pinhole camera. Many interesting projects can be done with either the paper or pinhole camera.

WORKING WITH LIGHT-SENSITIVE PAPER

Light striking light-sensitive paper interacts with chemicals in the paper, creating an outline of any object placed on the paper—the portion of the paper beneath the object does not change color, since it is not exposed to light.

One such paper is available in museum shops and hobby shops, toy stores, and specialty shops

[125]

Photo 33. Light-sensitive paper can be used to produce images without a camera. In this image the surface area of various types of leaves can be compared.

like the Nature Company. Another type of paper, called Diazo paper, is sold by the Bruning Company, whose address is listed in Appendix B.

Light-sensitive paper can be used to study insect wings; leaf damage caused by insects or atmospheric pollution; differences in the surface area of leaves; floral parts; feathers; and small skeletons. See Photo 33.

"Taking pictures" with light-sensitive paper is economical and results in life-size images. The image forms rapidly and can be developed in minutes, enabling you to view the results quickly. You can easily make a new image if the results are not satisfactory. The final pictures can be stored. Of course, such paper can record an image only when the object touches the paper. A good article on the subject is "White Prints," by Rita A. Hoots, published in the January 1991 issue of *Science Teacher*, a magazine your science teacher may subscribe to.

When using any light-sensitive paper, you will need to work in a low-light area. Cut the paper to a size large enough to hold the specimen. Place the paper on a piece of cardboard for support. Carefully arrange the specimens on the paper. Cover with a piece of clear Plexiglas or glass to keep them flat and in position.

Now expose the arrangement to full sunlight. Develop according to the manufacture's instructions, which should be included with the paper when purchased.

PINHOLE CAMERAS—PHOTOGRAPHY WITHOUT LENSES

Variations of early cameras, known as pinhole cameras can be constructed today. Interestingly, pinhole cameras have been used to great artistic advantage by some twentieth-century professional photographers, including Ansel Adams, one of the greatest photographers of all time.

Figure 4 shows a film cartridge pinhole camera, which can be made using a 126-size film cartridge. Make the box attached to the cartridge from light cardboard and use rubber bands to hold it in place. The metal needs to be somewhat thicker than heavy aluminum foil; the metal sheets used

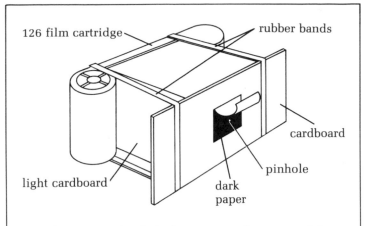

Figure 4. A pinhole camera for use with roll film. This type of design allows multiple photos to be made before the film is processed.

in printer's linotype work well. Punch a small hole in the metal and cover the hole with dark paper until ready to take a picture. Use a coin or key to advance the film.

Figure 5a shows a pinhole camera made from an oatmeal box. Spray the inside of the container with flat black paint. Cut a hole in one end, poke a pinhole in a piece of lightweight metal, and cover the hole in the container with the metal piece. Tape a flap of stiff paper over the metal to block light until you are ready to take a picture.

In a darkroom, cut a piece of print paper to snugly fit the lid and "load" it into the lid. See Figure 5b. Place the lid securely on the container before leaving the darkroom.

Instructions for building other pinhole cam-

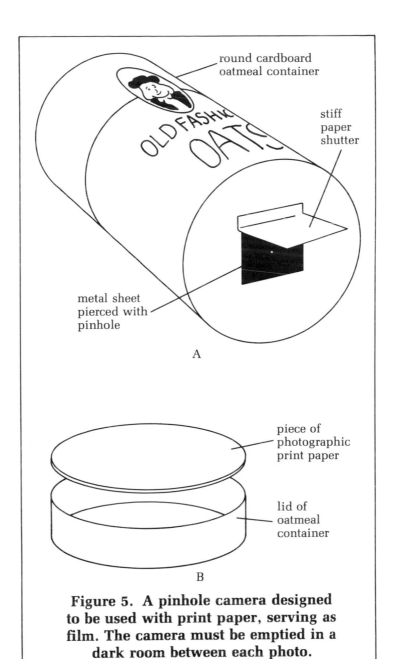

round cardboard oatmeal container

stiff paper shutter

metal sheet pierced with pinhole

A

piece of photographic print paper

lid of oatmeal container

B

Figure 5. A pinhole camera designed to be used with print paper, serving as film. The camera must be emptied in a dark room between each photo.

eras can be found in a number of science books and articles, some of which are listed in the "For Further Reading" section, at the back of this book.

Once the camera is built, you will have to decide whether to use photographic print paper or regular negative film as your film. Using photographic print paper requires that you know how to work in a darkroom and also how to develop each print after the photo has been taken. You can't take a sequence of pictures. Negative film can be hand developed and printed, or developed and printed at a commercial lab.

Work with photographic paper as follows. To load the camera, go into the darkroom, cut a piece of print paper to fit the side of the camera opposite the pinhole, carefully seal the camera, then leave the darkroom to take the picture. After taking the picture, return to the darkroom, unload the camera, and process the image. This image will be a negative. Its dark tones will be recorded as white and its light tones as dark.

If you choose to make a true print, you again will need to work in the darkroom with a safe light. Cut a second piece of print paper to cover the first image. Wet both pieces of paper with water and join the two so that the shiny side of the emulsions of both pieces of paper touch. Hold the papers so that the negative image is facing—and close—to the room's light. Turn on the light for a couple of seconds. Separate the two pieces of paper and process the new print the same way you did the negative.

When working with regular film, carefully place the roll in the homemade camera. Advance the film manually between exposures. Process the exposed roll yourself or at a lab. The advantage of hand printing is that it enables you to adjust for incorrect exposures.

Pinhole cameras are a bit clumsy to use, but their simplicity and economy make them worth experimenting with. They lend themselves well to studies of light and image formation.

PROJECTS

USING LIGHT-SENSITIVE PAPER

1. Trees growing along highways are subjected to large amounts of airborne chemicals. Compare the leaf size of trees growing beside a highway with that of trees of the same species growing at a distance from the highway. Which location seems more suitable for maximum photosynthetic production?

2. Compare the leaves of plants afflicted with leaf-cutting insects with leaves of healthy plants of the same type. Is the photosynthetic capability of the injured plants affected?

3. Compare the ratio of body weight to wing surface of various insects. Which insects produce the most lift in flight?

4. Compare the size of a tree's leaves from a variety of locations on the tree (for example, near the top, on an outside edge, close to the trunk). Using surface area as your guide, find out which part of the tree if any is the most photosynthetically productive. Does pruning affect leaf size over a growing season?

5. Aphids are leaf-sucking insects commonly found on rose bushes. Compare the bud development of two rose bushes—one infested with aphids, the other healthy.

6. The south side of a home or school building receives more sunlight than the north side. This increased amount of light causes the soil and air temperatures to be higher than at the north side. These small areas, such as the south and north sides, are known as microclimates. Explore the impact of microclimates on plant life surrounding your home or school building.

7. Sewing machine needles are available in a variety of sizes. Using an assortment of those needles to make a pinhole camera, explore the relationship between needle size and the resulting exposure time. Will the size of the opening affect picture clarity?

8. Some projects may require a broader field of vision or bringing distant objects closer. Develop a "wide angle" or "telephoto" pinhole camera to meet these needs.

9. Photograph litter patterns on your school grounds. Develop a program to foster student awareness to alleviate the situation.

APPENDIX A

BUILDING A SMALL AQUARIUM FOR CLOSE-UP PHOTOGRAPHY

To construct your own aquarium, first decide what size you will need. Then contact a glass shop and have the necessary glass pieces cut. To protect your hands during assembly, request that the edges be sanded. Remember the edges of newly cut glass may still be sharp. Wear leather gloves when handling pieces of glass and be very careful. During construction, cover your work surface with newspaper. Before actual assembly, join all pieces together with tape to check for proper fit. Once fit is assured, you are ready to begin assembly.

The bottom piece of glass is the foundation for your aquarium. Place a thin line of silicone aquarium sealer along the top edge of one of the long dimensions of your aquarium bottom glass. Place the front piece of glass in the sealant and carefully align the edges. Have someone hold this piece in

Photo 34. Goldfish in an aquarium ready
to be photographed. Note how construction
paper was used to line the back piece of glass.
This will remove distracting backgrounds that
might detract from the photo.

place while you carefully place a small bead of
sealant along the side edge of the glass you have
just placed and the adjacent side of the bottom
glass. Slide the end piece of your tank into the
sealant and secure the glass in position using a
couple of pieces of masking tape.

[134]

Secure all sides with masking tape while the sealant dries, usually overnight. Use a soft cloth to remove extra sealant before it dries. A razor blade will remove unwanted dried sealant.

After the aquarium has cured overnight, remove the tape and fill it with water to check for leaks. To plug a seeping seam, place a small amount of sealant on your fingertip, reach into the tank to the place where water seems to be flowing from, and seal the leak. Repeat this process until all leaks have been stopped.

Be sure to keep both large surfaces of glass free from smudges of sealant as these will be your photographic surfaces.

Once complete, your aquarium is ready for photography. See Photo 34.

APPENDIX B

MAIL-ORDER SOURCES

OF SUPPLIES

SCIENTIFIC SUPPLY COMPANIES

Carolina Biological Supply Co.

Main Office and Laboratories
2700 York Road
Burlington, NC 27215
800-334-5551
919-584-0381 (in North Carolina)

Powell Laboratories Division
19355 McLoughlin Boulevard
Gladston, OR 97027
800-547-1733
503-656-1641 (in Oregon)
Biology/Science

Central Scientific Company
1122 Melrose Ave.
Franklin Park, IL 60131
800-262-3626

Chem Shop
1151 So. Redwood Pl.
Suite 105
Salt Lake City, UT 84104

Edmund Scientific Co.
101 E. Gloucester Pike
Barrington, NJ 08007-1381
609-573-6250
609-547-3488

LaMotte Chemical Products Company
P.O. Box 329
Chestertown, MD 21620
800-344-3100
301-778-3100 (in Maryland)

NASCO Science
901 Janesville Ave.
Fort Atkinson, WI 53538-1901
414-563-2446

NASCO West
1524 Princeton Ave.
Modesto, CA 95352-3837
209-529-6957

Orion Telescope Center
2450 17th Avenue, P.O. Box 1158
Santa Cruz, CA 95061
800-447-1001
800-443-1001 (in California)

Ward's Natural Science Establishment
P.O. Box 1712

Rochester, NY 14603
P.O. Box 1749
Monterey, CA 93940
800-962-2660

PHOTOGRAPHIC EQUIPMENT AND SUPPLIES

Bruning
2788 East Vernon Avenue
Vernon, CA 90058
(source of Diazo paper)

Calumet Photographic
890 Supreme Drive
Bensenville, IL 60106
800-225-8638

Camera Brokers Plus
188 14th Street N.W.
Atlanta, GA 30318
800-462-5425
404-892-5522 (in Atlanta)

Porter's Camera Store
P.O. Box 628
Cedar Falls, IA 50613-9986
800-553-2001

Spiratone
3045 West Liberty Ave.
Pittsburgh, PA 15216
800-221-9695

MODEL ROCKETS

Estes Industries
1295 H St.
Penrose, CO 81240

FOR FURTHER READING

BOOKS AND ARTICLES

GENERAL

Beller, Joel. *So You Want to Do a Science Project!* New York: Arco, 1986.

Bleifeld, Maurice. *Experimenting with a Microscope.* New York: Franklin Watts, 1988.

Headstrom, Richard. *Adventures with a Microscope.* New York: Dover, 1977.

Pasachoff, Jay M. *Peterson First Guides, Astronomy.* Boston: Houghton Mifflin, 1988.

Rainis, Kenneth G. *Nature Projects for Young Scientists.* New York: Franklin Watts, 1989.

Science Project Photography. Burlington, N.C.: Carolina Biological Supply Company, 1987.

Tocci, Salvatore. *How to Do a Science Project.* New York: Franklin Watts, 1986.

UNESCO. *700 Science Experiments for Everyone.* New York: Doubleday, 1962.

ANIMAL AND PLANT CARE

Hooft, Jan, and Bayly, Robert F. *The Carolina Guide to Plants and Terraria*. Burlington, N.C.: Carolina Biological Supply Company, 1981.

Koch, William J. *Plants in the Laboratory*. New York: Macmillan, 1973.

Orlans, F. Barbara. *Animal Care from Protozoa to Small Mammals*. Menlo Park, Calif.: Addison-Wesley, 1977.

PHOTOGRAPHY

Banks, Michael M. "Aerial Photography with Model Rockets." *Science PROBE!*, November 1990, pp. 94–101.

Bauer, Erwin. *Outdoor Photography*. New York: Dutton, 1974.

Covington, Michael. *Astrophotography for the Amateur*. Cambridge, England: Cambridge University Press, 1985.

Davidson, Michael W. "Microscapes: Fascinating Photos with a Simple Microscope." *Photographic*, April 1991, pp. 92–96.

Fordyce, Robert P. *Science Project Photography*. Burlington, N.C.: Carolina Biological Supply Co., 1987.

Fuller, Thomas F. "A Portable Copy Stand." *Photographic*, September 1987, pp. 72–73.

Hedgecoe, John. *The Book of Photography*. New York: Knopf, 1981.

Images of the World. Washington, D.C.: National Geographic Society, 1981.

Lewis, Dan. *The How to Build Your Own Photographic Equipment Book*. Douglas, Wy.: Wyoming Naturalist, 1991.

McDonald, Joe. *A Practical Guide to Photographing American Wildlife*. Emmaus, Pa.: Foxy-Owl Publications, 1983.

Moldvay, Albert. *The National Geographic Photographer's Field Guide*. Washington, D.C.: National Geographic Society, 1981.

PINHOLE CAMERAS AND RELATED TOPICS

Goodwin, Peter. *Engineering Projects for Young Scientists*. New York: Franklin Watts, 1987.

Granderson, S. Irving. "The Pinhole Camera Revisited." *Science and Children*, February 1987, pp. 6–8.

Hoots, Rita A. "White Prints." *The Science Teacher*, January 1991, pp. 16–19.

How to Make and Use a Pinhole Camera. Kodak pamphlet AA-5.

Luke, Michael. "Trying Your Hand at a Handmade Camera."
Science and Children, February 1987, pp. 9–12.
Riss, Helphers Pam. "Smile You're Inside My Oatmeal Box."
Science Scope, September 1990, pp. 24–26.

HISTORY

Boorstin, Daniel J. *The Discoverers: A History of Man's Search to
Know His World and Himself*. New York: Random House,
1983.
Ford, Brian J. *Single Lens—The Story of the Simple Micro-
scope*. New York: Harper & Row, 1985.
Magner, Lois N. *A History of the Life Sciences*. New York:
Marcel Dekker, 1979.

KODAK PUBLICATIONS

Basic Scientific Photography. Book N-9.
Close-up Photography. Book N-12A.
Composition. AC-11.
Improve Your Environment. AC-26.
Infrared Films. Book N-17.
Photography in Your Science Fair Project.
AN-18.
Photography in Your Science Fair Project.
AT-20.
Photography Through the Microscope. Book P-2.
Tips for Photographing Your Trip Abroad.
AC-17.

PERIODICALS

Outdoor Photographer
Peterson's Photographic
The Science Teacher

INDEX

Page numbers that are italicized refer to illustrations.

[142]

EDUCATION